GCSE 9-1

ENGLISH
LANGUAGE & LITERATURE
REVISION GUIDE FOR
ALL EXAM BOARDS

Richard Durant
Cindy Torn

Authors Richard Durant, Cindy Torn
English series editor Richard Durant
Editorial team Haremi Ltd
Series designers emc design ltd
Typesetting York Publishing Solutions Pvt. Ltd., INDIA
Illustrations York Publishing Solutions Pvt. Ltd., INDIA
App development Hannah Barnett, Phil Crothers and Haremi Ltd

Designed using Adobe InDesign
Published by Scholastic Education, an imprint of Scholastic Ltd, Book End, Range Road, Witney, Oxfordshire, OX29 0YD
Registered office: Westfield Road, Southam, Warwickshire CV47 0RA
www.scholastic.co.uk

Printed by Bell & Bain Ltd, Glasgow
© 2017 Scholastic Ltd
1 2 3 4 5 6 7 8 9   7 8 9 0 1 2 3 4 5 6

British Library Cataloguing-in-Publication Data
A catalogue record for this book is available from the British Library.
ISBN 978-1407-16917-0

Note from the publisher
Please use this product in conjunction with the official specifications and the sample assessment materials for your GCSE 9–1 English Language and GCSE 9–1 English Literature exam board. Ask your teacher if you are unsure where to find them.

Contents

Acknowledgements

The publishers gratefully acknowledge permission to reproduce the following copyright material:

Text permissions

p.11: *Lord of the Flies*, William Golding, Faber & Faber, 1954; p.14: *Small Island*, Andrea Levy, Headline Review, 1996, p.337; p.20: *Atonement*, Ian McEwan, Vintage, 2002, pp.4–5; p.24: *Sons and Lovers*, DH Lawrence, Wordsworth, 1913; pp.29–30: *Brick Lane: A Novel*, Monica Ali, Scribner, 2003; p.48: *Tracks*, Louise Erdrich, Penguin Putnum, 1988; p.48: *Farenheit 451*, Ray Bradbury, Ballantine Books, 1953; p.48: *The Crow Road*, Iain Banks, Little, Brown, UK, 1992; p.48: *The Great Gatsby*, F Scott Fitzgerald, Scribner, 1925; p.48: *City of Glass*, Paul Auster, Sun & Moon Press, 1985; p.48: *Adventures of Huckleberry Finn*, Mark Twain, Chatto & Windus, 1885; p.48: *The Towers of Trebizond*, Rose Macaulay, Collins, 1956; p.48: *A Farewell to Arms*, Ernest Hemingway, Scribner, 1929; p.49: *Never Let Me Go*, Kazuo Ishiguro, Faber & Faber Ltd, UK, 2005; p.57: 'Why it's time to let go of "Let it Go"', by Rae Earl, theguardian.com, 17 December 2014, © Guardian News & Media Ltd 2017; p.59: 'Why it's time to let go of "Let it Go"', by Rae Earl, theguardian.com, 17 December 2014, © Guardian News & Media Ltd 2017; p.61: Letter to the President of the United States, 1852, attributed to Chief Seattle; p.66: *The Book of Household Management*, Mrs. Isabella Beeton, S. O. Beeton Publishing, London, 1861; p.67: Warm spiced cauliflower and chickpea salad with pomegranate seeds, from *Simply Nigella* by Nigella Lawson. Published by Chatto & Windus, reprinted by permission of The Random House Group Limited. pp.71–2: Letter to the President of the United States, 1852, attributed to Chief Seattle; p.94: *Never Let Me Go*, Kazuo Ishiguro, Faber & Faber Ltd, UK, 2005; p.110: *Macbeth*, William Shakespeare, Act 5 Scene 5, Cambridge School Shakespeare, Cambridge University Press; p.111: *Macbeth*, William Shakespeare, Act 5 Scene 5, Cambridge School Shakespeare, Cambridge University Press; p.118: *Strange Case of Dr Jekyll and Mr Hyde*, Robert Louis Stevenson, Longmans, Green & Co., UK, 1886; p.125: *Lord of the Flies*, William Golding, Faber & Faber, 1954; p.126: *Lord of the Flies*, William Golding, Faber & Faber, 1954; p.127: *An Inspector Calls*, JB Priestley, 1945; p.128: *Lord of the Flies*, William Golding, Faber & Faber, 1954; p.128: *The Curious Incident of the Dog in the Night-Time*, Mark Haddon, Jonathan Cape, UK, 2003; p.129: *An Inspector Calls*, JB Priestley, 1945; p.130: *Lord of the Flies*, William Golding, Faber & Faber, 1954; p.138: 'War Photographer' from *New Selected Poems* by Carol Ann Duffy. Published by Picador, 2009. © Carol Ann Duffy. Reproduced by permission of the author c/o Rogers, Coleridge & White Ltd., 20 Powis Mews, London, W11 1JN; p.141: 'Neutral Tones', Thomas Hardy, 1867; p.144: 'Catrin', from *Collected Poems*, Gillian Clarke, Carcanet Press, 1997, © Carcanet Press Limited, Manchester, UK, reprinted by kind permission; p.149: 'A Memory', Lola Ridge, 1918; Throughout: Assessment objectives, Department of Education, subject content and assessment objectives © Crown Copyright 2013 Open Government Licence.

Photo permissions

p.32: Vadim Ponomarenko/Shutterstock; p.36: mbuckley98@googlemail.com/Shutterstock; p.38: Cedric Weber/Shutterstock; p.43: Cedric Weber/Shutterstock; p.45: Heldinho/Shutterstock; p.46: Heldinho/Shutterstock; p.117: lady-luck/Shutterstock.

Every effort has been made to trace copyright holders for the works reproduced in this book, and the publishers apologise for any inadvertent omissions.

How to use this book

This Revision Guide has been produced to help you revise for your 9–1 GCSEs in English Language and English Literature. Broken down into sections it presents the information in a manageable format. Written by subject experts to match the new specifications, it revises all the content you need to know before you sit your exams.

The best way to retain information is to take an active approach to revision. Don't just read the information you need to remember – do something with it! Transforming information from one form into another and applying your knowledge through lots of practice will ensure that it really sinks in. Throughout this book, you will find lots of features that will make your revision an active, successful process.

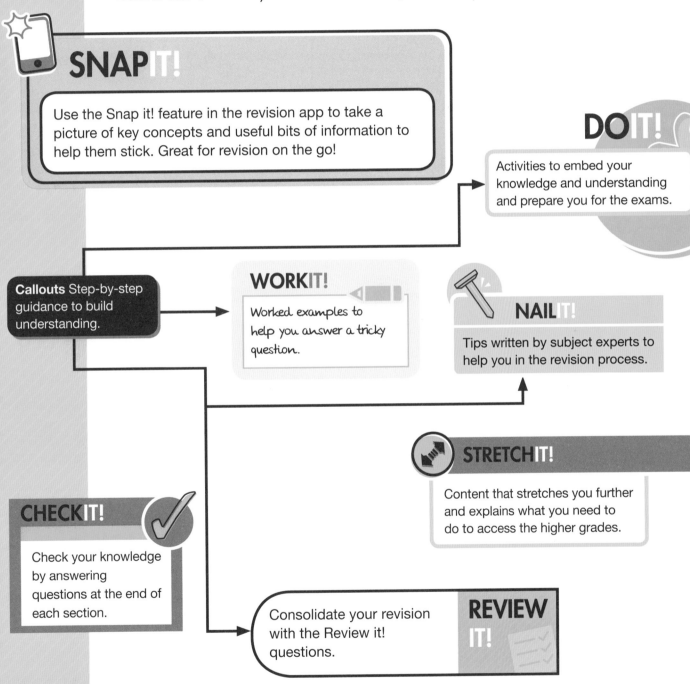

SNAPIT!

Use the Snap it! feature in the revision app to take a picture of key concepts and useful bits of information to help them stick. Great for revision on the go!

DOIT!

Activities to embed your knowledge and understanding and prepare you for the exams.

Callouts Step-by-step guidance to build understanding.

WORKIT!

Worked examples to help you answer a tricky question.

NAILIT!

Tips written by subject experts to help you in the revision process.

STRETCHIT!

Content that stretches you further and explains what you need to do to access the higher grades.

CHECKIT!

Check your knowledge by answering questions at the end of each section.

REVIEW IT!

Consolidate your revision with the Review it! questions.

Use the All Boards English Language and English Literature Exam Practice Book alongside the Revision Guide for a complete revision and practice solution. Packed full of exam-style questions for each section, along with full practice papers, the Exam Practice Book will get you exam ready!

HOW TO REVISE!

PLAN YOUR REVISION

Get ahead by planning your revision!

Work out the **time** you have available for revising.

Think about when you work at your best. Are you a morning or an evening person?

Use your **revision app** to put together a revision timetable.

Allocate **MORE TIME** for the topics you struggle with.

Revision works best in **SMALL BURSTS**, so keep sessions **SHORT AND SWEET**!

Remember to allow time to **PRACTISE** applying what you have revised.

LOOK AFTER YOURSELF

Help your brain by looking after your whole body!

Take regular **breaks** from revising – your brain needs time to digest information in order to retain it.

★ HOTEL ★

Keep **hydrated** by drinking plenty of water – dehydration stops your brain from working at its full capacity.

Regular **exercise** helps stimulate the brain and will help you relax.

Get plenty of **sleep**, especially the night before an exam.

EAT WELL and limit unhealthy snacks – your brain needs fuel for memory and concentration.

Find methods of **relaxation** that work for you throughout the revision period.

BE PREPARED!

Limit potential stress on the day of an exam by getting everything you need ready the night before.

30

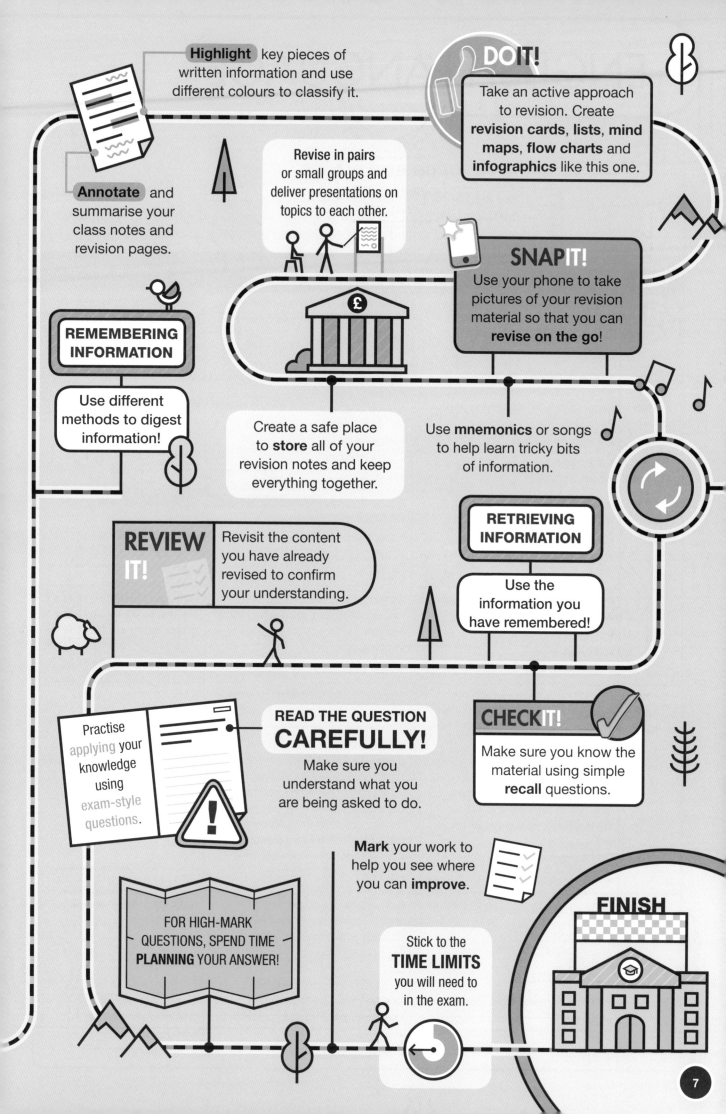

Highlight key pieces of written information and use different colours to classify it.

Annotate and summarise your class notes and revision pages.

Revise in pairs or small groups and deliver presentations on topics to each other.

DO IT!

Take an active approach to revision. Create **revision cards**, **lists**, **mind maps**, **flow charts** and **infographics** like this one.

SNAP IT!

Use your phone to take pictures of your revision material so that you can **revise on the go**!

REMEMBERING INFORMATION

Use different methods to digest information!

Create a safe place to **store** all of your revision notes and keep everything together.

Use **mnemonics** or songs to help learn tricky bits of information.

RETRIEVING INFORMATION

Use the information you have remembered!

REVIEW IT!

Revisit the content you have already revised to confirm your understanding.

Practise applying your knowledge using exam-style questions.

READ THE QUESTION CAREFULLY!

Make sure you understand what you are being asked to do.

CHECK IT!

Make sure you know the material using simple **recall** questions.

Mark your work to help you see where you can **improve**.

FOR HIGH-MARK QUESTIONS, SPEND TIME **PLANNING** YOUR ANSWER!

Stick to the **TIME LIMITS** you will need to in the exam.

FINISH

ENGLISH LANGUAGE

Introduction and advice

There are two English Language GCSE exams. Each of the exams is in two parts: reading and writing. One exam will focus on fiction, the other on non-fiction, but the reading and writing skills being tested are similar in both papers.

Exam board	Exam	Section A: Reading	Section B: Writing
AQA	Paper 1: Explorations in Creative Reading and Writing • 1 hour 45 minutes • 80 marks • 50% of GCSE	Answer four questions on part of a 20th/21st-century literature fiction text. • 40 marks • 25% of GCSE	Write a description or a narrative (story). • 40 marks • 25% of GCSE
AQA	Paper 2: Writers' Viewpoints and Perspectives • 1 hour 45 minutes • 80 marks • 50% of GCSE	Answer four questions on two linked non-fiction texts. • 40 marks • 25% of GCSE	Write to present a viewpoint. • 40 marks • 25% of GCSE
Edexcel	Paper 1: Fiction and Imaginative Writing • 1 hour and 45 minutes • 64 marks • 40% of GCSE	Answer four questions on an unseen 19th-century fiction extract. • 24 marks • 15% of GCSE	A choice of two writing tasks. The tasks are linked by a theme to the reading extract. • 40 marks • 25% of GCSE
Edexcel	Paper 2: Non-fiction and Transactional Writing • 2 hours • 96 marks • 60% of GCSE	Answer seven questions on two thematically linked, unseen non-fiction extracts. • 56 marks • 35% of GCSE	A choice of two writing tasks. The tasks are linked by a theme to the reading extracts. • 40 marks • 25% of GCSE
Eduqas	Paper 1: 20th Century Literature Reading and Creative Prose Writing • 1 hour 45 minutes • 80 marks • 40% of GCSE	Answer five structured questions on one literary prose extract from the 20th century. • 40 marks • 20% of GCSE	A choice of four creative writing tasks. • 40 marks • 20% of GCSE
Eduqas	Paper 2: 19th and 21st Century Non-fiction Reading and Transactional/Persuasive Writing • 2 hours • 80 marks • 60% of GCSE	Structured questions based on two extracts of high-quality non-fiction writing, one from the 19th century, the other from the 21st century. • 40 marks • 30% of GCSE	Two transactional/persuasive writing tasks. • 40 marks • 30% of GCSE
OCR	Paper 1: Communicating Information and Ideas • 2 hours • 80 marks • 50% of GCSE	Answer four questions on two unseen non-fiction texts, one of which is a 19th-century text. • 40 marks • 25% of GCSE	A choice of two non-fiction writing tasks. • 40 marks • 25% of GCSE
OCR	Paper 2: Exploring Effects and Impact • 2 hours • 80 marks • 50% of GCSE	Answer four questions on two literary texts from the 20th or 21st century. • 40 marks • 25% of GCSE	A choice of two original creative writing tasks. • 40 marks • 25% of GCSE

Fiction: Reading

Introduction and advice

In the reading section of the fiction exam you will be give an extract from a story or novel and some questions to answer on the text.

You will be tested against the following assessment objectives for reading:

	• Identify and interpret explicit and implicit information and ideas. • Select and synthesise evidence from different texts.
	Explain, comment on and analyse how writers use language and structure to achieve effects and influence readers, using relevant subject terminology to support their views.
	Compare writers' ideas and perspectives, as well as how these are conveyed, across two or more texts.
	Evaluate texts critically and support this with appropriate textual references.

Differences between the exam boards

SNAP IT! Personalise it! Fiction: Reading

Board	
AQA	☞ Marks: 40 ☞ Time: 1 hour ☞ The extract will be a literature fiction text. It will be drawn from either the 20th or 21st century.
Edexcel	☞ Marks: 24 ☞ Time: 1 hour ☞ The extract will be from fiction written before 1900. (The extract will have been written after 1900 in the other boards' exams.)
Eduqas	☞ Marks: 40 ☞ Time: 1 hour ☞ You will be given one prose extract from literary prose from the 20th century.
OCR	☞ Marks: 40 ☞ Time: 1 hour ☞ Paper 2 focuses on fiction (it is Paper 1 for the other boards). There will be two extracts from different texts, and one of these might be literary non-fiction, such as autobiography or travel writing. You will be asked to briefly compare the texts. Both texts will be 20th or 21st-century prose.

NAIL IT!

When you open the exam paper, read the questions first and then read the extract. That way you will read with a strong sense of purpose, and that will help you to concentrate. Spend 15 minutes reading and preparing the text.

NAIL IT!

Notice how many marks are given for each question. Don't spend long on questions that carry very few marks. Leave yourself enough time for questions that carry a lot of marks.

AO1: Identifying and interpreting information and ideas

Assessment objective 1 tests your ability to identify information and ideas that are actually there in front you.

Below are the sorts of AO1 questions you will be asked:

- List four things that show that the narrator was nervous.
- List five things you learn about why Sadiq was angry.
- Identify one word that shows that Callum is in a hurry.
- Identify the phrase which explains why everyone is too hot to move.

These sorts of questions have right answers. There are no marks for being clever and complicated: you just need to be clear, simple and accurate.

Differences between the exam boards

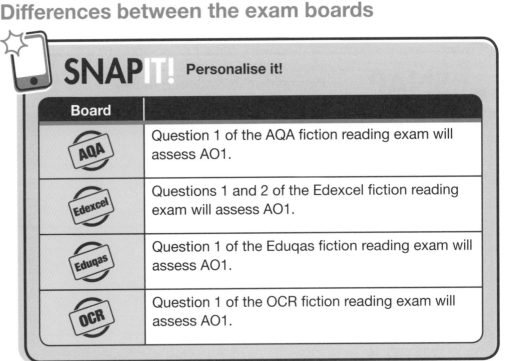

SNAPIT! **Personalise it!**

Board	
AQA	Question 1 of the AQA fiction reading exam will assess AO1.
Edexcel	Questions 1 and 2 of the Edexcel fiction reading exam will assess AO1.
Eduqas	Question 1 of the Eduqas fiction reading exam will assess AO1.
OCR	Question 1 of the OCR fiction reading exam will assess AO1.

Identifying facts and other details in the text

Here is the first sentence from William Golding's novel, *Lord of the Flies*:

> The boy with fair hair lowered himself down the last few feet of rock and began to pick his way toward the lagoon.

Here are some facts we can find in this sentence:

The boy's hair was fair in colour.

He is climbing down some rock.

He then goes towards a lagoon.

We can also work out (or '**deduce**') something from how he approached the lagoon. Golding narrates his movement with these words: he 'began to pick his way'. 'Pick' suggests that he was moving carefully and having to choose his direction at every step. This might suggest that the terrain was difficult to walk through.

So the information given to us as readers comes in two forms:

- Details that are right there in front of us. These are **explicit** details.

- Details that are suggested or implied. These are **implicit** details.

Implicit details have to be worked out by the reader. For example, in the opening to *Lord of the Flies* the boy's hair 'was plastered to his forehead'. It doesn't say that his hair was sticky with sweat, but we can work this out for ourselves.

Here is the opening to *Lord of the Flies*. Some words and phrases that suggest the weather was hot are highlighted:

> The boy with fair hair lowered himself down the last few feet of rock and began to pick his way toward the lagoon. Though he had taken off his school sweater and trailed it now from one hand, his grey shirt stuck to him and his hair was plastered to his forehead. All round him the long scar smashed into the jungle was a bath of heat. He was clambering heavily among the creepers and broken trunks when a bird, a vision of red and yellow, flashed upwards with a witch-like cry; and this cry was echoed by another.

Below is one student's response to the question:

> List four things from this part of the text that show that the weather was hot.

WORKIT!

1 He had taken off his sweater.

2 He had fair hair.

3 There is so much here that makes me think of heat. For example, the word 'smashed' sounds angry and anger is often connected to heat. We sometimes say someone did something in the 'heat of anger', so smashed is angry and violent and therefore hot.

4 His hair is sticky with sweat.

NAILIT!

Even when you have to work out information for yourself, the exam markers want your answers to be simple and straightforward.

NAILIT!

Read the extract very closely. If you just skim and scan you will miss the detail.

DOIT!

Imagine you are a teacher. Write a **short** note to the student who gave the four answers in the Work it!. Explain why answers 2 and 3 are wrong and therefore get no marks.

11

Inferring and interpreting information and ideas in texts

As we have already seen, there are – broadly speaking – two sorts of information:

1 Things you can almost copy directly from the source.

2 Things that are implied in the source so that you have to draw a conclusion from the detail. For example, 'his hair was plastered to his forehead' does not actually tell you that the day is hot, but we can infer it – we can work it out for ourselves. You may know this as 'reading between the lines' because the detail is not actually written anywhere on the page – it's suggested to the reader.

NAILIT!

If you are unsure of something you are inferring, then just add a simple explanation or some simple evidence from the extract to back up your inference.

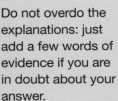

NAILIT!

Do not overdo the explanations: just add a few words of evidence if you are in doubt about your answer.

DOIT!

To explore the difference between knowing and inferring, find some pictures of people you don't know – perhaps in magazines or newspapers – and jot down things we can clearly observe about the person (for example, gender), and things we might infer about them from their picture (for example, they are angry).

Think about how our assumptions might affect our inferences. For example, if we don't like the look of a person, we might infer that they are untrustworthy. However, we would probably be wrong.

CHECKIT!

1 Which one of the following things is being tested in Question 1?

- Evaluating the effect of the writing.
- Finding the information.
- Analysing the structure of the source.
- Exploring the writer's choice of language.

2 What is the difference between explicit and implicit information?

AO2: How writers use language and structure to influence readers

Assessment objective 2 tests your ability to explain how writers use language and structure to achieve effects and influence readers. AO2 is tested through 'How' questions which focus on how the writer has expressed their ideas, how they have described characters or a scene or event, and how they have organised their writing. For these questions you will need to consider:

- vocabulary (word level – detailed, close up)
- sentence styles and forms (sentence level – broader focus)
- structure and organisation (whole text level – the big picture).

Differences between exam boards

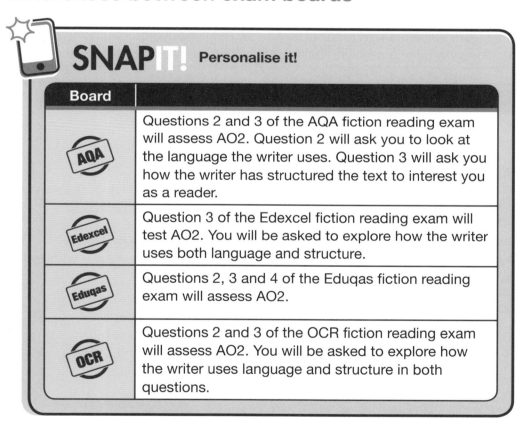

SNAPIT! **Personalise it!**

Board	
AQA	Questions 2 and 3 of the AQA fiction reading exam will assess AO2. Question 2 will ask you to look at the language the writer uses. Question 3 will ask you how the writer has structured the text to interest you as a reader.
Edexcel	Question 3 of the Edexcel fiction reading exam will test AO2. You will be asked to explore how the writer uses both language and structure.
Eduqas	Questions 2, 3 and 4 of the Eduqas fiction reading exam will assess AO2.
OCR	Questions 2 and 3 of the OCR fiction reading exam will assess AO2. You will be asked to explore how the writer uses language and structure in both questions.

NAILIT!

AQA is the only exam board that sets a question that is only about structure.

Language choices and their effects

Part of assessment objective 2 assesses your ability to explain and comment on how a writer has chosen their language to have an effect on you. You will have to use relevant subject terminology and evidence to support your views.

Here is what those key words mean:

SNAPIT!

Word	Explanation
Language	You need to think about words the writer has **chosen**. All of us express things in different ways: we make **choices**. We choose our words carefully so that we use the right ones for the effect we want to have. Writers choose *very* carefully. The writer's choice of words – and the writer's choice of sentence forms – is what we mean by the writer's **language**.
Effect	This is about how the reader responds to the writer's words: what does the reader think of/how does the reader **feel**? Writers choose their words to affect the reader in particular ways.
Your views	These are your beliefs about what the writer is trying to do and how they are trying to do it.
Evidence	These are the details from the text that you choose in order to support the views you put forward. Evidence can be in the form of quotations.
Subject terminology	These are technical words about language. English subject terminology includes words and phrases like sentence, verb, simile, rhetorical question.

Below is a short extract from the novel *Small Island* by Andrea Levy. Read the extract and the comments. The comments explain how key words about language choice and effect might be relevant to the extract.

Language: the second sentence is not a full sentence. It is not a complete statement. This is also true of sentences 4, 5 and 6.

The effect of these 'chopped up', incomplete sentences is that we get a sense of how surprised the narrator is. It is as though she cannot easily take in what has happened.

"
I'd have recognised it anywhere, the back of Bernard's neck. Bony and scrawny like the back of a heel with his ears sticking out. Seeing me there on the pavement he came towards me. A hat. A white collar. A gaberdene mac* – every button done up and the belt too. He lifted his hat when he reached me, formal, courteous, as if this was a casual meeting. And I was collapsed, sitting on the pavement because my husband whom I hadn't seen for near five years had just approached me. And I said, 'Bernard. You've been away a long time.'

And all he said was, 'Indeed.'

Just that. In-bloody-deed.

Small Island, Andrea Levy

* A sort of raincoat
"

DOIT!

Read the *Small Island* text again. Look very carefully at the last line:

"
Just that. In-bloody-deed.
"

How does the writer use language here to show the narrator's feelings? Write up to six lines to explain your ideas.

Use these rules:

- Analyse the effect of the writer's **choice** of language.
- Explain your views, and use some evidence.
- Use some **subject terminology**.

What is written in the comments is, of course, only a '**viewpoint**', but it is explained, and some details in the text – some **evidence** – is pointed out.

Mark scheme for language (AO2)

When the examiners mark your answers, they refer to **mark schemes**. These schemes are made up of 'band descriptors' rather like the ones below.

SNAPIT! Mark scheme for language (AO2)

Mark scheme level	Band 2 descriptors (Roughly GCSE grades 2–3)	Band 3 descriptors (Roughly GCSE grades 4–6)	Band 4 descriptors (Roughly GCSE grades 7–9)
The student's answer...	• shows some appreciation of language choices • comments on the effects of language choices • uses some relevant evidence, including quotations • tries to use some subject terminology.	• shows clear appreciation of language choices • explains the effects of some language choices • uses relevant evidence (including quotations) from different parts of the text • uses helpful, relevant subject terminology.	• examines language choices with insight and precision • closely analyses the effects of language choices • carefully chooses a variety of evidence, including quotations • uses a range of precise and helpful subject terminology.

Look again at the ending to the short extract from the novel *Small Island* by Andrea Levy:

> Just that. In-bloody-deed.

How does the writer use language here to show the narrator's feelings?

You should have written your own answer in response to the activity on page 14. Here is another student's answer with some comments:

> Some accurate subject terminology – 'sentences', 'verbs'.

WORKIT!

is swer uld be aced w in nd 3.

Neither of these 'sentences' are real sentences. They don't contain verbs. They don't make sense really – not on their own. They sound more like someone talking than writing. The effect of that is that the words sound sarcastic and abrupt. They even sound rude and the swearing makes the rudeness even stronger.

> Clear explanation of the effect of the writer's choice of words. No quotations, although details are pointed out.

Here are two more answers:

WORKIT!

Student answer A

The narrator uses a mild swear word – 'bloody' – to show that she is cross with Bernard. She keeps things short too. This might show that she is fed up.

Student answer B

Clearly the narrator is annoyed with Bernard. We get this impression because her made-up word, 'In-bloody-deed', contains a swear word and it echoes Bernard's words sarcastically. 'Just that' is an incomplete sentence – as though Bernard's ridiculous explanation doesn't deserve anything more.

DOIT!

Look at the two student answers above, and at your own answer. Compare each answer with the band descriptors you've just looked at in the mark scheme. Would you give each answer a Band 2, 3 or 4? Explain your thinking.

Use a table like the one shown to analyse the three answers.

Answer	How it compares with the mark scheme descriptors	Mark band
A	The student chooses one relevant quotation and gives a very brief explanation of what it tells us about the narrator, although nothing is said about how it affects the mood...	
B		
My answer		

Sentence styles and forms

One aspect of language choice that many students ignore is sentence forms. You will notice that one of the answers you have just looked at does begin to consider the **effect** of sentence styles and forms: 'Just that' is an incomplete sentence – as though Bernard's ridiculous explanation doesn't deserve anything more.

All writers vary their word order and the lengths and sorts of sentence for effect. This is what examiners calls 'sentence forms'.

In the extract below, the writer is trying to use varied sentence forms to affect the way the reader responds to the narrator. The sentence forms help the narrator to show his feelings.

DOIT!

Make some notes on the extract. Identify:

- different sorts of sentence (simple, compound, complex)
- varied lengths of sentence
- word order in sentences
- the effect of these on the reader.

" I left the 'welcome' desk and dragged my bags angrily for the next half hour up to my room. 'Just up the stairs,' I'd been assured. There were two flights of steep steps to negotiate before I could reach my assigned hovel on the third storey of the dilapidated building. Miguel was there already. Spread thinly across three-quarters of the cramped space were his pitiful belongings, and he was coughing extravagantly into the remaining quarter. My quarter. "

Below is what one student wrote about the extract:

WORKIT!

The first sentence has two clauses, separated by the word 'and'. The last ten words of the first sentence consists of three adverbials giving more information about the verb 'dragged': 'angrily' (how); 'for the next half hour' (when) and 'up to my room' (where). This list of adverbials deliberately drags the sentence out and emphasises the physical dragging that the narrator is doing.

NAILIT!

Don't just spot sentence features: explain how the chosen features convey meaning and effect.

DOIT!

Add to the comments on this answer, and then finish off the answer. Try to:

- keep the same Band 4 quality
- use the bullet points in the Do it! on page 16 to guide you.

Here is the first part of a Band 4 response to the *Small Island* extract:

WORKIT!

By the end of the extract the narrator's negative attitude towards Bernard is plain. Clearly the narrator is annoyed with Bernard. We get this impression because her made-up word, 'In-bloody-deed', contains a swear word and it echoes Bernard's words sarcastically. 'Just that' is an incomplete sentence – as though Bernard's ridiculous explanation doesn't deserve anything more. The incompleteness of the sentence also implies that the narrator can't be bothered either. You can imagine her turning to you and saying, 'Just that,' as though they want you to notice that Bernard has just confirmed what the narrator has been telling you about him. 'Just that' has an informal, oral quality. It's almost as though the narrator has said to the reader, 'There you go. Just like I was saying.' However, this weary, contemptuous attitude is present throughout the extract. Even at the beginning...

> This feature – use of an incomplete sentence – is explored in depth.

> Relevant subject terminology – informal, oral – is identified and its effect is explored.

> Impact on reader is described.

To gain the highest marks when writing about language choices you need to:

- identify a range of language features and explore them in detail (write a lot about a little)
- explain the effect of the language features on the reader (what do they make you think of, how do they make you feel?)
- use relevant subject terminology as part of your explanation
- choose the best quotes and embed them where you can.

How writers use structure to achieve effects

Assessment objective 2 also assesses your ability to explain and comment on how a writer has structured (organised) their writing to have an effect on you. You must use subject terminology when explaining your views.

Structure is about the things that a writer uses to make their writing a **coherent** (or joined-up and understandable) whole. The structure of a piece of writing includes those features that hold it all together and make it work. Texts in this exam will typically be structured into a sequence of paragraphs which together exert an influence on the reader. Without structure, writing becomes random, hard to follow and ineffective. You must be able to identify structural features, and then explain their effects.

Before you review your understanding of structural features in writing, it is worth considering what we mean by the structure of a number of different things.

For example, if we dismantled a fridge and put all the bits in a bag, it would no longer be a fridge, even though every part was still there: it would no longer have the structure of a fridge.

Similarly, if we took an extract from a novel and jumbled up its words (or even its letters), we would no longer have an extract from a novel, even though it was still 'all there': the extract would no longer have a meaningful structure.

Here are some of the structural features of a fridge:

- door hinges to connect the door and allow it to open and close
- a motor in the right place and connected correctly
- a light that usefully comes on when the door opens
- right angles at its corners.

Narrative fiction – like anything else – has features that hold it together, make it 'work', and make it recognisable as narrative fiction. There is no official list of these features, but some common structural features you might find in an extract from a novel include:

DOIT!

Write down some structural features for each of the following things:

a a bike

b a school

c a film

d an extract from a novel.

SNAPIT!

Structural feature	Explanation
Information put into a particular order (sequence)	For example, information about a character might be given to us in this order: appearance, behaviour, some background.
Dialogue to reveal character, move the narrative on, etc.	Writers often use direct speech (dialogue) so that we can 'hear' what characters sound like. It can bring them to life for us.
Narrative chronology	Most stories are told in the order they happened (their chronology). Some stories (and films) are structured around dramatic events, with shifts into the past and future to explain those events.
Narrative shifts	For example, from small, close-up details to larger and larger ones, or the opposite.
Repetition – of words, phrases, ideas, images, etc.	Repetition can be a sort of thread that connects parts of the text together.
Changing/ developing focus	For example, from description of a view, to description of the immediate scene, to the thoughts of a character.
Extended images	A writer might describe a person or place in a certain way, and then develop this image over a few lines (or even chapters).
A particular style, tone or mood	A large part of a story (or all of it) might have a particular style, tone or mood: for example, humorous, sad, mocking, tense, and so on. Tone is the attitude of the writer or narrator towards what they are writing about.
Narrative voice and perspective	Often a story is told from one character's point of view – their perspective. Sometimes it is the author's 'voice' that we can almost hear.
Paragraphs	Changes of paragraph are often used to signal shifts: in time, place, topic, action, and so on. Topic sentences can be used to signal a changing or developing theme.
Summaries, introductions, conclusions	For example, an event or character might be introduced, developed, and some sort of conclusion reached.
Genre	Many stories fit a particular genre: horror, romance, science fiction, for example. The typical features of the genre may be part of the story's structure.

DOIT!

Think of all the structural features you have learned about during your English course. Write down a few, and give brief explanations for each one.

NAILIT!

Learn your list of structural features. Look out for examples of them in everything you read. Choose random parts of novels and stories and see if you can identify structural features in them.

DOIT!

- What impression of Briony do you get?
- What other structural features has the writer used?
- How does each feature help to build the overall impression of Briony?

Read this short extract from the novel *Atonement* by Ian McEwan. Here, a character called Briony is introduced to us. Notice how the writing is organised. Notice its tone, and other **structural features**, and how these give us a strong impression of Briony.

> She was one of those children possessed by a desire to have the world just so. Whereas her big sister's room was a stew of unclosed books, unfolded clothes, unmade bed, unemptied ashtrays, Briony's was a shrine to her controlling demon: the model farm spread across a deep window ledge consisted of the usual animals, but all facing one way – towards their owner – as if about to break into song, and even the farmyard hens were neatly corralled. In fact, Briony's was the only tidy upstairs room in the house. Her straight-backed dolls in their many-roomed mansion appeared to be under strict instructions not to touch the walls; the various thumb-sized figures to be found standing about her dressing table – cowboys, deep-sea divers, humanoid mice – suggested by their even ranks and spacing a citizen's army awaiting orders.
>
> *Atonement*, Ian McEwan

The impression we are given of Briony as a character (a person) is the overall structural feature of this extract.

Mark scheme for structure (AO2)

The mark scheme for structure is nearly the same for language, except that the focus is on **structural features** rather than **language choices**. The answer must give evidence – not necessarily quotations – and use subject terminology accurately.

SNAPIT! Mark scheme for structure (AO2)

Mark scheme level	Band 2 descriptors (Roughly GCSE grades 2–3)	Band 3 descriptors (Roughly GCSE grades 4–6)	Band 4 descriptors (Roughly GCSE grades 7–9)
The student's answer...	• shows some appreciation of structural features • comments on the effects of structural features • uses some relevant evidence • tries to use some subject terminology.	• shows clear appreciation of relevant structural features • explains the effects of some relevant structural features • uses different forms of relevant evidence • uses helpful, relevant subject terminology.	• examines relevant structural features with insight and precision • closely analyses the effects of relevant structural features • carefully chooses a variety of evidence • uses a range of precise and helpful subject terminology.

DO IT!

Re-read the extract from *Atonement* (page 20) and look again at the mark scheme for structure.

Now read the three different explanations of impressions we get of Briony below. One of the answers is in Band 2, one is in Band 3, and one is in Band 4. Decide which is which, and write down why.

WORKIT!

Student answer A

The writing is very persuasive for the reader. We aren't given any chance to see Briony unclearly: how she is, is very clear indeed. One way the writer does this is by using strong words about Briony's obsession right through the extract: she is 'possessed'; she has a 'controlling demon'; her dolls are 'under strict instructions'; her models are in 'ranks' awaiting 'orders'. All the words make us see Briony as an extreme controller. Also, the writer uses…

Student answer B

The writing is structured almost like a formal argument: it starts by asserting that Briony's strongest motivation is to 'have the world just so'. In other words, Briony wants to control and organise her world. The next few lines give examples of this to convince the reader that Briony has this 'controlling demon' inside her. Halfway through the extract, the phrase 'In fact' introduces an even more emphatic persuasion that Briony is a controller. This emphasis of Briony's controlling and ordering behaviour is strengthened by the use of contrast – with her sister's 'stew' of untidiness and everyone else's room being untidy as well. Another structural feature used by the writer in giving a clear picture of Briony is…

Student answer C

The writer keeps repeating words that have the same beginnings – un – unclosed, unfolded, and so on. This repeating seems to bang into the reader's mind this picture of the mess in Briony's sister's room, and of course Briony's room isn't like that at all. This repeating feature makes this picture very clear and strong. All the words about Briony's habits with her things are also very strong and that makes it really definite that Briony is a controller. You can't really disagree. So for example she 'coralls' her model animals, and her model people are in ranks and wait for orders.
Briony is also…

STRETCHIT!

To gain the highest marks when writing about structure and its effects you need to:

- write about a number of different sorts of structural features
- explore some aspects of structure and investigate the effects of those aspects
- refer to carefully chosen examples
- use relevant subject terminology purposefully.

Language and structure

SNAPIT! Personalise it!

☞ AQA is the only exam board that sets a question that is only about **structure** (Question 3).

☞ The other three exam boards set questions that ask about language as well as structure. To gain the most marks in these questions you have to write about both language and structure in a balanced way.

☞ Of course, it is often hard to tell language and structural features apart: they work together to have particular **effects** on the reader.

CHECKIT! ✓

1 Look back over the advice you have read about answering questions with a language focus.

 a Without looking at this book, make a list of the five key words that are related to questions on language choices.

 b Next to each word (or phrase) explain why it is important.

 Here is an example of a key word and its explanation:

Word or phrase	Explanation and thoughts
Effect	The impact on the reader: how the chosen words make the reader feel or react. It is important to explain what the effect is (or effects are).

2 Without looking at this book, make a list of at least ten structural features from memory. Write an explanation next to each feature.

3 Which one of the following three things could count as a structural feature?
 a spelling b repetitions c exclamation marks.

4 List three reasons for starting a new paragraph.

5 What image is being extended in the following sentence?

> " He quacked his way through the next song, flapping his arms
> helplessly, wishing he could float away unnoticed. "

6 What is meant by 'tone' in fiction?

7 What is meant by the 'structure' of a fiction extract?

AO4: Evaluating texts critically

The final question in the reading section of the fiction paper will test assessment objective 4. It will focus on how much or how well the author influences us. Your job is to evaluate the writing. You will be asked about all, or part of, the extract.

You will need to evaluate ideas, events, themes and settings as well as providing a critical overview of the text and a judgement on it as a whole. These are the sorts of questions you will be asked:

- Evaluate how successfully the writer creates suspense.

- To what extent do you agree that the writer creates a very clear and engaging picture of the characters?

- How far do you agree that we are made to feel sorry for the narrator?

NAILIT!

AQA, Eduqas and OCR will provide you with a reader reaction statement in this question.

Differences between the exam boards

SNAPIT! **Personalise it!**

Board	
OCR	The final question in the fiction reading section will also assess AO3. 12 marks are awarded for AO4 and 6 marks are awarded for AO3. AO3 is not assessed by any of the other boards in the fiction reading section of the exam. For information about the AO3 criteria, see pages 64–72.
Edexcel	You will not be given a reader reaction statement in this question.

The evaluation question will ask you to consider how successful the writer has been in **engaging** the reader. Partly this is about giving a thoughtful **personal response**. Partly it is about choosing **evidence** from the text to support your response. You need to appreciate what the writer is trying to do, and how they are trying to do it. Be critical in an analytical way, which means carefully considering the text, its language, and its tone and style. The golden rules for this question are:

- read and understand the question carefully

- think about what impact or influence the writer is trying to have on you, the reader

- think about what is good (and perhaps less good) about the writing

DOIT!

Make a poster containing six frames – one for each of the golden rules. Write a rule in each box and draw a simple symbol or picture to help you remember each one.

- don't get carried away with your own feelings about the text: keep your distance
- use quotes from the text to support your thoughts
- evaluate ideas, events, themes and settings, and provide a critical overview of the text and a judgement on it as a whole.

Responding to the text

Evaluation questions assess how you react to the text. You must show that you are sensitive to the meaning, tone and mood.

Below is a typical text extract for the evaluation question. The extract is taken from near the end of a novel by DH Lawrence, published in 1913. Paul is about to go away, but Miriam had been hoping he would stay.

> She stood before the mirror pinning on her hat. How bitter, how unutterably bitter, it made her that he rejected her sacrifice! Life ahead looked dead, as if the glow were gone out. She bowed her face over the flowers—the freesias so sweet and spring-like, the scarlet anemones flaunting over the table. It was like him to have those flowers.
>
> He moved about the room with a certain sureness of touch, swift and relentless and quiet. She knew she could not cope with him. He would escape like a weasel out of her hands. Yet without him her life would trail on lifeless. Brooding, she touched the flowers.
>
> 'Have them!' he said; and he took them out of the jar, dripping as they were, and went quickly into the kitchen. She waited for him, took the flowers, and they went out together, he talking, she feeling dead.
>
> She was going from him now. In her misery she leaned against him as they sat on the car. He was unresponsive.
>
> Where would he go? What would be the end of him? She could not bear it, the vacant feeling where he should be. He was so foolish, so wasteful, never at peace with himself. And now where would he go? And what did he care that he wasted her? He had no religion; it was all for the moment's attraction that he cared, nothing else, nothing deeper. Well, she would wait and see how it turned out with him. When he had had enough he would give in and come to her.
>
> *Sons and Lovers*, DH Lawrence

Below are some sample evaluation and response questions:

- Who do you like more – Miriam or Paul? Why?
- What are the differences between Miriam's and Paul's personalities?
- What does Miriam fear?
- What is important to Paul?
- What is Miriam's attitude towards Paul?

This sort of question requires you to 'enter' the text and to share the experiences of the characters.

DO IT!

Think about the response questions and jot down your answers. Look carefully at the details in the text that influence your responses.

Then think of two or three other possible reactions to the text. Write them down. Decide which of these reactions you think are the most reasonable and explain why.

Here is an example evaluation question on the *Sons and Lovers* extract on the previous page. Notice how it starts with a reader reaction statement:

> Here is a reader reaction. You must use it as the focus for what you write about the extract.

A student, having read this section of the text, said:

'The writer really makes you feel the depth of Miriam's distress. The writer takes you right inside her heart and mind.'

To what extent do you agree?

In your response you could:

- write about **your own impression** of Miriam's thoughts and feelings
- **evaluate** how the writer has created these thoughts and feelings
- support your opinions with **references to the text**.

> This is the actual question: how much do you agree with the reaction?

> These prompts are there to help you structure and develop your answer. The key ideas in these prompts are:
>
> 'your own impression'
>
> 'evaluate'
>
> 'references to the text'.

NAIL IT! Edexcel

If your exam board is Edexcel, you will not be given a reader reaction statement in this question.

Key ideas in the evaluation question

Your own impression: you need to develop an impression – a response. Explore the **effect** of the writing as a reader – what does the extract make you think of? How does it make you feel?

Evaluate: to **evaluate** you need to decide how good (in other words how successful) the writing is. Explore **how** the writing makes you feel the way it does – how has the author been successful in making you feel this way?

References to the text: refer to the text to support the relevant points you make. Choose some very short quotations and explain how they are relevant and the effect they might have on a reader.

Look again at this extract from a novel:

> I left the 'welcome' desk and dragged my bags angrily for the next half hour up to my room. 'Just up the stairs,' I'd been assured. There were two flights of steep steps to negotiate before I could reach my assigned hovel on the third storey of the dilapidated building. Miguel was there already. Spread thinly across three-quarters of the cramped space were his pitiful belongings, and he was coughing extravagantly into the remaining quarter. My quarter.

DO IT!

Answer the following two questions, making some references to the text:

- What impression do we get of the narrator and his feelings? (Your own impression.)
- What is good about the writing? (Evaluate.)

Of course, the way that this extract has been written influences our impressions of the narrator. It would be possible to rewrite the extract so that it contains roughly the same information in the same order, but gives a different impression of the narrator. For example, what if the extract began like this?

> Smiling, I turned from the welcome desk and carried my bags calmly up to my room.

We would probably get a different impression of the narrator: he or she seems calm and satisfied.

DOIT!

1 Try rewriting the whole extract on page 25 three times. Keep the same information but try to create three different impressions of the narrator:

- dangerous
- nervous
- confident.

2 Find short extracts in novels you have read. Decide what impression the reader gets about the character or the situation in the extract. Rewrite the extracts so that the reader gets different impressions.

By doing this you are experimenting with:

- how a writer creates impressions in the reader
- the quality of the writing
- how details in the text create particular impressions.

Mark scheme for evaluating texts critically (AO4)

SNAPIT! Mark scheme for evaluating texts critically (AO4)

Mark scheme for evaluating texts critically (AO4)

Mark scheme level	Band 2 descriptors (Roughly GCSE grades 2–3)	Band 3 descriptors (Roughly GCSE grades 4–6)	Band 4 descriptors (Roughly GCSE grades 7–9)
The student's answer...	• tries to make some comments that evaluate the text • refers to a relevant example from the text • refers to some of the writer's techniques • uses a couple of helpful quotations.	• includes a clear evaluation • gives examples that support and clarify points • helpfully explains the effects of some of the writer's techniques • uses helpful quotations from different parts of the text.	• critically evaluates the text in a detailed way • gives examples from the text to explain views convincingly • analyses effects of a range of the writer's choices • justifies points with relevant quotations from different parts of the text.

Here is one student answer to the question on page 25, with some comments about how it might meet some of the descriptors.

WORKIT!

So the writer does keep saying how deep Miriam's despair and depression is – 'bitter', 'dead'...

Some relevant quotations to support views.

... but we also get this impression from the contrast with Paul's behaviour and attitude: he has 'a certain sureness of touch' and he is compared with a weasel that is impossible to hold onto because it is so lively. This contrast of characters makes the reader wonder whether this separation was inevitable.

Paul seems to be completely unaware as to how Miriam is feeling, making him seem shallow and uncaring in comparison to the depth of Miriam's 'brooding' unhappiness.

Examples from the text to convincingly explain these views.

This part of the answer seems to be in Band 3 (although the whole answer might be better or worse than Band 3).

 STRETCHIT!

To get the highest possible marks for evaluation questions, you need to keep asking yourself, 'How is this writer trying to hold my interest?' Simply analysing the extract, spotting methods and features in a mechanical way, will not get you to the top of the mark scheme. You also need to evaluate the text critically. That does not mean giving it a mark out of ten, or even saying how good it is, but it does mean being able to explain what you particularly like about a text and why.

CHECKIT! ✓

1 Write down five important things you have learned about how to answer an evaluation question.

2 Below are parts of answers to the question on *Sons and Lovers* from page 25. Put these three answers into a rank order from best to worst. Within the answers, find examples of advice and rules for an evaluation question being kept or broken.

Student answer A

It says 'brooding' and that shows she is thinking hard and a bit miserable about it. It's definite – we know just how she is feeling because the writer says it. We know she is deep in her thoughts. Later on it says 'misery' when she is leaning on him. Again we know exactly how deep she feels.

Student answer B

So the writer does keep saying how deep Miriam's despair and depression is – 'bitter', 'dead' – but we also get this impression from the contrast with Paul's behaviour and attitude: he has 'a certain sureness of touch' and he is compared with a weasel that is impossible to hold onto because it is so lively. This contrast of characters makes the reader wonder whether this separation was inevitable.

Student answer C

I don't really like this writing and I can't get into it because Miriam seems so hopeless and a bit pathetic. On the other hand, perhaps that means I am right inside Miriam's heart and mind. Although the author is telling the story (he is the narrator), we see things from Miriam's point of view, so we are sort of with her. For example, when it says 'It was like him to have those flowers' it doesn't say that the narrator says this: it's like Miriam has suddenly become the narrator!

3 Which one of the following questions is an evaluation question?

a How well does the writer create comedy in this extract?

b What does the character do for a living?

c How does the writer use language to create tension in this extract?

The extracts in this section come from the beginning of Monica Ali's novel *Brick Lane*. Rupban is pregnant and plucking a chicken when she suddenly goes into labour. The local midwife arrives. The baby's name is Nazneen.

01 Identify and interpret information and ideas

1 How many minutes should you spend reading the questions and the text extract (source)?

2 What should you do before you read and while you read the text?

3 What skills are being assessed in questions testing AO1 in the fiction reading section?

> " --
>
> Hamid ran from the latrine, although his business was unfinished. He ran across the vegetable plot, past the towers of rice stalk taller than the tallest building, over the dirt track that bounded the village, back to the compound and grabbed a club to kill the man who was killing his wife. He knew it was her. Who else could break glass with one screech? Rupban was in the sleeping quarters. The bed was unrolled, though she was still standing. With one hand she held Mumtaz's shoulder, with the other a half-plucked chicken.
>
> Mumtaz waved Hamid away. 'Go. Get Banesa. Are you waiting for a rickshaw? Go on, use your legs.'
>
> "

4 Write down four things that show that characters have a sense of urgency. Keep your information as simple as possible.

02 How writers use language and structure to influence readers

5 What skills are being assessed in questions testing AO2 in the fiction reading section?

> Banesa arrives but pronounces the baby dead.
>
> " --
>
> 'See your daughter,' Banesa said to Rupban. 'Perfect everywhere. All she lacked was someone to ease her path to this world.' She looked at Cheepy-cheepy lying next to the bereaved mother and hollowed her cheeks; a hungry look widened her eyes slightly although they were practically buried in crinkles. It was many months since she had tasted meat, now that two young girls (she should have strangled them at birth) had set up in competition.
>
> 'Let me wash and dress her for the burial,' said Banesa. 'Of course I offer my service free. Maybe just that chicken there for my trouble. I see it is old and stringy.'
>
> "

6 What impression of Banesa do we get from these lines? How does the writer give us this impression? (Consider the writer's choice of language, including sentence forms.)

7   Write down at least ten examples of structural features.

> Now the baby comes back to life.
>
> " -
>
> Mumtaz took hold of Nazneen, who was still dangling by the ankle, and felt the small, slick torso slide through her fingers to plop with a yowl onto the bloodstained mattress. A yowl! A cry! Rupban scooped her up and named her before she could die nameless again.
>
> Banesa made little explosions with her lips. She used the corner of her yellowing sari to wipe some spittle from her chin. 'This is called a death-rattle,' she explained. The three women put their faces close to the child. Nazneen flailed her arms and yelled, as if she could see this terrifying sight. She began to lose the blueness and turned slowly to brown and purple. 'God has called her back to earth,' said Banesa, with a look of disgust.
>
> - "

8   Explain how the writer has structured the text to interest you. Consider how the writer has used some particular structural features.

 Evaluating texts critically

NAIL IT!

Create a plan for Question 11 before you answer it.

9   What is being tested in evaluation questions?

10 Look back over all three extracts.

- How do you feel about one or more of the characters?
- How well do you think the writer has created the scene?
- How successful has the writer been in making the scene interesting?

11
Evaluate the way Banesa is presented in these extracts.

You should write about:

- your own thoughts and feelings about how Banesa is presented in the extracts
- how the writer has created these thoughts and feelings.

Fiction: Writing

Introduction and advice

In the writing section of the fiction exam, you will be tested against the following assessment objectives:

	• Communicate clearly, effectively and imaginatively, selecting and adapting tone, style and register for different forms, purposes and audiences. • Organise information and ideas, using structural and grammatical features to support coherence and cohesion of texts.
	Candidates must use a range of vocabulary and sentence structures for clarity, purpose and effect, with accurate spelling and punctuation.

Differences between the exam boards

SNAPIT! Personalise it! Fiction: Writing

Board	
AQA	☞ Paper 1: Section B ☞ Marks: 40 ☞ Time: 45 minutes ☞ You will have a choice of two tasks. ☞ AQA will sometimes offer a description-only task. ☞ One of the writing choices will be based on a picture. ☞ The tasks will always link to the theme of the reading stimulus in the reading paper.
Edexcel	☞ Paper 1: Section B ☞ Marks: 40 ☞ Time: 45 minutes ☞ You will have a choice of two tasks. ☞ One of the writing choices will be based on a picture.
Eduqas	☞ Paper 1: Section B ☞ Marks: 40 ☞ Time: 45 minutes ☞ You will have a choice of four tasks.
OCR	☞ Paper 2: Section B ☞ Marks: 40 ☞ Time: 1 hour ☞ You will have a choice of two tasks.

The exam paper will ask you to write a narrative – either a story that is fiction or something that has really happened in your life. You will be expected to include descriptions in your writing. You will have a choice of tasks and you must choose **one** of them. The writing task will appear as Section B on the paper. Here are examples of the sorts of writing task you might be asked to carry out:

> Write the dramatic ending to a mystery story.

> Write a description of a place that is special to you.

> Write a description suggested by this picture.

> Describe an exciting day in your life. Focus on your thoughts and feelings at the time.

NAIL IT!

Only Edexcel and AQA will offer a writing task based on an image.

STRETCH IT!

The best writing will tend to be more ambitious with its use of sentence variety and vocabulary. The focus of this paper is on creativity, and so high marks will go to writing that is accurate and well controlled, but also original.

Make sure you leave at least 45 minutes to do the writing task. In other words, don't spend too much time on Section A of the exam paper. You should aim to write at least two sides of average-sized handwriting – but remember the quality of your writing is more important than quantity.

There are 40 marks for the writing task:

- 24 marks for communication and organisation

- 16 marks for vocabulary, sentence structure, spelling and punctuation (VSSSP).

Communication (AO5) is about your ideas and how you express yourself so that you 'connect' with your reader (audience). You should communicate clearly, effectively and imaginatively and use tone, style and register that are appropriate for the given form, purpose and audience.

Organisation (AO5) is about how you structure your content, for example, with paragraphs, discourse markers, openings and closings. You should organise information and ideas, using structural and grammatical features to support coherence and cohesion.

VSSSP is about spelling, punctuation and grammar, and about using effective sentence length and structure and vocabulary. Use a range of vocabulary and sentence structures for clarity, purpose and effect with accurate spelling and punctuation. You can lose a lot of marks for being inaccurate, so be careful. (See the VSSSP section starting on page 93.)

Different types of writing task

Broadly speaking, the writing tasks in the fiction writing section of the exam fall into five categories. Not all of the exam boards offer all of the categories.

> **SNAP IT!** Personalise it! Fiction writing tasks
>
> | Category | Exam board |
> |---|---|
> | Descriptive writing with a visual stimulus | AQA |
> | Descriptive writing without a visual stimulus | AQA |
> | Narrative writing with a visual stimulus | AQA   Edexcel |
> | Narrative writing – the opening to a story | AQA |
> | Narrative writing – a complete story | AQA   Edexcel   Eduqas   OCR |

This book will cover each of the five categories in turn. You will find it useful to work through all of the categories, even if they are not offered by your exam board, as the tasks will help you build your AO5 skills and contain information relevant to all five categories.

Writing a complete story includes two slightly different sorts of text type:

- **fiction** (a story)
- **autobiography** (a story of something that happened to you).

Of course, good narrative writing will always include descriptions, and descriptions of events are a form of narrative. It is worth being clear about the typical key features of different forms of writing:

NAIL IT!

Fiction and autobiography narratives might need slightly different treatments. However, what you write will need to interest a reader who does not know you. You have more chance of doing this if you plan the outline of your writing before you start to write.

SNAPIT!

Fiction	Autobiography/recounting real events	Purely descriptive (AQA only)
• Written in the past tense • Action important • Dialogue (direct speech) • Characters and scenes created by the writer	• Written in the past tense • Action often less important than feelings, reactions, lessons learnt by the writer	• Written in the present tense • Action not important AQA

DOIT!

Read the three pieces of writing. Which one is narrative fiction? How do you know?

NAILIT!

Make sure you spend between five and ten minutes planning:

- your ideas
- how your ideas will be organised
- the sort of words and phrases that will be effective and appropriate.

NAILIT!

The AO5 mark scheme accounts for 60% of the marks for writing. Vocabulary, sentence structure, spelling and punctuation take up the remaining 40% of the writing marks. See the section on VSSSP later in this book.

These are **typical** features, but the forms can overlap. For example, descriptive writing can include descriptions of actions, and occasionally fiction narratives are written in the present tense.

> **A**
>
> Nestling among rich green pine groves and backed by the spectacular snow-capped San Antonio mountains, Sudorno Hotel is a jewel in the island's crown. At night it gleams like a diamond as it catches the moonlight over the tranquil bay.

> **B**
>
> She caught a glimpse of the hotel through the fading light. It shone like a jewel. She crouched into the cover of the thick undergrowth and stealthily made her way towards her target. It was certainly a perfect, tranquil place, but no guest would get much sleep that night.

> **C**
>
> On the best day of my life I was excited from the moment I woke up. The moment I opened my eyes I almost gasped with the thrill of knowing where I would be going that day. I flung back my bed covers and flipped myself out of my top bunk, landing perfectly on my feet before I leaped into the bathroom.

Mark scheme for communication and organisation (AO5)

Whatever category the writing task belongs to, it is meant to help you to write creatively. The skills involved in writing the task are always the same, and every task will be marked against the same mark scheme. On page 35 is a simplified version of the mark scheme for you to refer to as you revise.

SNAPIT! Mark scheme for communication and organisation (AO5)

Mark scheme level	Band 2 descriptors (Roughly GCSE grades 2–3)	Band 3 descriptors (Roughly GCSE grades 4–6)	Band 4 descriptors (Roughly GCSE grades 7–9)
AO5 Communication	• is mainly clear in expression • keeps trying to match register to purpose, form and audience • chooses words with some care • uses some linguistic devices.	• is clear, effective and engaging throughout • mainly matches register to purpose, form and audience • precisely chooses words and phrases for deliberate effect • uses varied linguistic devices for impact.	• wins the reader over and holds their interest throughout • precisely matches register to purpose, form and audience • uses a wide and adventurous vocabulary • carefully chooses linguistic devices for effect throughout.
AO5 Organisation	• uses suitable ideas that have some variety and sometimes link together • uses some paragraphs and discourse markers • uses some other structural features (for example, deliberate repetition, topic sentences).	• uses varied ideas, linking them well • carefully organises paragraphs around well-chosen discourse markers • uses structural features for deliberate impact.	• is highly structured and developed around a range of dynamic and complex ideas • is highly coherent and fluent in organisation, incorporating discourse markers in a natural way • uses a range of structural features skilfully and creatively.

DOIT!

Look at the mark scheme and decide which areas you will need to concentrate on to move your writing towards the next band up. Write these down as personal targets for improvement.

✓ CHECKIT!

1 How many marks are available for the imaginative and creative writing task?

2 How many marks are available for communication and organisation?

3 How many writing tasks will be on the paper for you to choose from?

4 Which sorts of writing might you have to choose from in this writing exam?

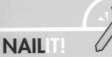
Question type 1: descriptive writing with a visual stimulus

Here is an example of a descriptive question with a visual stimulus.

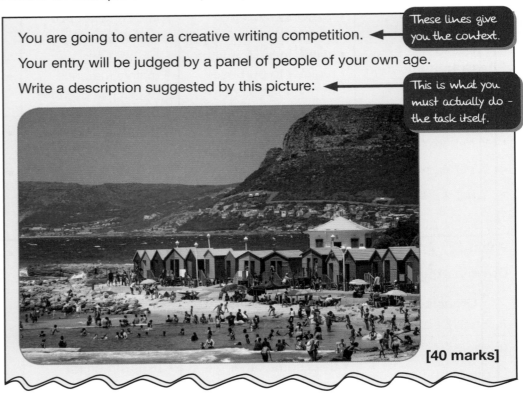

You are going to enter a creative writing competition. ← *These lines give you the context.*

Your entry will be judged by a panel of people of your own age.

Write a description suggested by this picture: ← *This is what you must actually do – the task itself.*

[40 marks]

Planning and generating ideas

The question tells us that the purpose for the writing is a competition entry and the audience is a group of people your age. However, as they are going to judge this entry you need to impress them. In the exam instructions on the front of the paper you are instructed to 'write in full sentences'. This tells you that you should write in Standard English (no text-speak or emojis) and you must make sure that your sentences are formed and punctuated correctly.

Look at the picture above.

One method of planning and structuring your description is to think of yourself looking at the scene. Imagine yourself to be a camera, one that can record what is seen and heard – but can also include other senses too. As you observe this scene, you can break it down into **five phases**:

1. **Set the scene.** This is where you create a wide-angled shot which gives a sense of the whole picture.

2. **Draw in other senses**. Sounds might work especially well here, but you could also describe smell or touch.

3. **Zoom in on one part of the scene**. Describe it in close detail.

4. **Find a contrast within the picture**. If it is a busy street, is there part of the picture where it is quiet?

5. **Back to the big picture.** Decide how you will return to the whole picture. How has the scene changed since the opening section? Has time moved on?

You should plan your ideas in response to the picture using a table like the one below, which relates to the example task on page 36. The prompts are there to help your thinking as you begin to generate your ideas. You should add questions that you find helpful as you use this method. Remember the prompts are sections of your description and sections may be one or more paragraphs each.

Phase	Notes – ideas and language
Phase 1: **Set the scene** • Where is it? or What is it? • What are the key colours? • Where are your eyes drawn to first of all? • What is the mood and atmosphere of this scene?	relaxing colourful rainbow foreground like a photo from a tourist brochure brooding background of cliff like a monster/evil whale?
Phase 2: **Draw in other senses** • What can you add to the plan here? • Smell? Sound?	
Phase 3: **Zoom in on one part of the scene** • What is the mood or atmosphere within the detail? • What is it that makes it interesting? Does it change the mood of the picture? (For example, a child crying on a sunny beach, someone walking alone along a crowded street.) • What realistic details can you add?	
Phase 4: **Find a contrast within the picture** • What can you add to the plan here? • What contrasting mood is suggested?	
Phase 5: **Back to the big picture** • How will you end your description? Will it end with the contrast or will you return to the whole picture? What changes will have taken place since the first section? • What realistic details can you add?	

DO IT!

Complete the rest of this table referring to the photo on page 36.

DO IT!

Find an interesting photograph in a magazine or online. Stick it on a sheet of paper and then prepare a description of it by filling in a table like the one here.

NAILIT!

Linguistic devices can help you to write successfully by making your writing vivid and believable. You can use figurative language in any of the five categories of tasks.

Linguistic devices: figurative language

The mark scheme for this question measures your ability to use a range of linguistic devices. Figurative devices (or imagery) are part of this group and can help you to write successful, descriptive pieces of writing.

- **Simile:** when two things are compared using **as** or **like** (for example, he fought **like** a lion).

- **Metaphor:** a figure of speech in which two things are compared, usually by saying one thing is another (for example, he **was** a lion in battle and he **roared** with anger).

- **Personification:** describing non-human objects using human characteristics: actions, body parts, emotions, and so on (for example, the hail hammered **angrily** against the **terrified** window).

Look at the picture of the castle below and read one student's description:

Notice how the student has repeated ideas and images. This is an extended metaphor. The student suggests that the castle is like an ageing warrior who is aching to rest its elderly structure.

WORKIT!

Exhausted by many lifetimes of cold and wind, the castle rests solidly in its landscape. Over the decades, it has crept towards the moat, desperate to paddle its stone and turrets. Glorious sunsets hide its ageing battlements as they silhouette in perfection, like a warrior against the horizon. But like those tourists who have been coming back year-by-year to soak up the sun, its skin has become cracked and worn by a weathered existence.

Here are some relevant descriptors that exam markers would use to judge the quality of writing. Look in particular at the final bullet point in each column.

Mark scheme level	Band 2 descriptors (Roughly GCSE grades 2–3)	Band 3 descriptors (Roughly GCSE grades 4–6)	Band 4 descriptors (Roughly GCSE grades 7–9)
AO5 Communication	• is mainly clear in expression • keeps trying to match register to purpose, form and audience • chooses words with some care • uses some linguistic devices.	• is clear, effective and engaging • mainly matches register to purpose, form and audience • chooses increasingly sophisticated words and phrases for effect • uses a range of appropriate linguistic devices.	• is convincing and compelling throughout • assuredly matches register to purpose, form and audience • manipulates the reader in subtle ways • uses a wide, ambitious vocabulary • uses carefully crafted linguistic devices throughout.

Here is what an exam marker wrote about the castle description on page 38:

```
This is an ambitious and confident description. It
engages the reader throughout. Its extended metaphor –
of the castle as an exhausted warrior – is well handled
and very believable. The simile that compares the
weathered castle to sunburn is also original (although
perhaps it goes too far).
```

✓ CHECKIT!

1 Write a few sentences to describe details from the castle scene on page 38. Use three types of imagery: simile, metaphor, personification.

2 In your sentences, are there images/ideas that are repeated or extended?

3 If not, which one is your favourite (strongest, most powerful) image/idea?

4 What would/could your extended metaphor be? How will this improve your writing?

Question type 2: descriptive writing without a visual stimulus

NAILIT!

AQA is the only exam board that offers a purely descriptive task in the exam. However, you should always consider the audience, purpose and form for any piece of writing you are asked to do.

Here is an example of a descriptive writing task without a visual stimulus.

> Your school or college is asking students to contribute some creative writing for its website.
>
> Describe an occasion when you faced a personal challenge.
> Focus on the thoughts and feelings you had at that time. **[40 marks]**

Planning

The **audience** here is the school community (students and teachers) but, as it is for the website, it will also have a wider audience of adults and even young people outside the school.

The **form** is creative writing for a school website.

The **purpose** is to describe an occasion, and – by implication – to show the school in a good light.

Preparing the question is always very important, and it is especially important for questions without a picture stimulus. Preparing the question means making sure you understand exactly what it is telling you to do, and making sure you have taken note of all the information in the question.

Here is how one student identified the key words in the question and planned their response:

NAILIT!

As part of your revision, it is good to annotate the question in the same way as the example in the Work it! That way you force yourself into a habit of looking very closely at every part of the task.

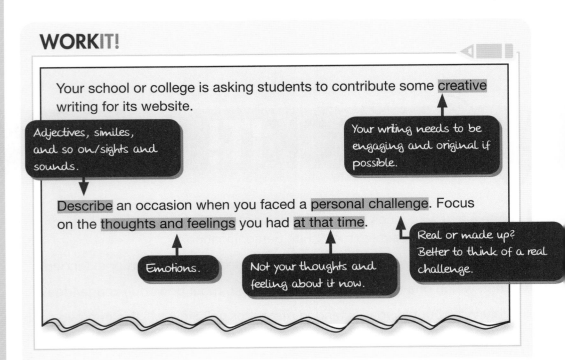

WORKIT!

Your school or college is asking students to contribute some creative writing for its website.

Adjectives, similes, and so on/sights and sounds.

Your writing needs to be engaging and original if possible.

Describe an occasion when you faced a personal challenge. Focus on the thoughts and feelings you had at that time.

Emotions.

Not your thoughts and feeling about it now.

Real or made up? Better to think of a real challenge.

This question is asking you to write about a personal challenge. However, it is asking you to describe your **thoughts** and **feelings**. Don't fall into the trap of just telling the story. This student has prepared the task very well by considering all its parts.

Below is the student's plan for the question. They have used **before**, **during** and **after** planning categories, and identified thoughts and feelings for each. This is a good example of producing a plan after having worked out exactly what the question is asking of you.

NAILIT!

Always be clear what the question is asking you.

WORKIT!

Personal challenge – my first day at a new school		
Before	Thoughts: Watching children in the playground – thinking that they look as if they belong there. Knowing that I will have to make new friends. Wishing that I didn't have to go. Thinking that if I ran away no-one would ever be able to find me.	Feelings: Missing the comfort of my old friends. Feeling nervous, apprehensive. Feeling as if my legs will not hold me. Feeling that it's all too noisy.
During	Thoughts: Walking into the classroom thinking that everyone is looking at me. Trying to remember names but knowing that I would forget and then they would all hate me. Thinking that the teachers seem different, more terrifying than my old school.	Feelings: Feeling out of control as if I'm on a rollercoaster. Getting an answer right and worrying that I would make a fool of myself.
After	Thoughts: It's over... It's over... It's over! Trying to think that it wasn't that bad – but really thinking it was. Thinking that I have to convince my mum that I am fine and happy.	Feelings: Feeling relieved but angry that I had to leave everyone I knew. Feeling happy that it was over but feeling dread that I had to go back. Understanding that it would get better. That I had started to make friends.

Here is another example question to help you to practise your AO5 skills:

> A leading breakfast cereal maker is offering a prize for the best description of the perfect breakfast. The judging panel will be made up of young employees of the company.
>
> Write a description of your perfect breakfast. This could be a breakfast you have had, or one you would like to have.

DOIT!

Prepare the question and then write a plan. You could (but you don't have to) use a before, during and after structure as shown above. You will need this plan later in this section of the book.

41

DO IT!

Write the opening paragraph of the 'perfect breakfast' task that you were given on page 41.

DO IT!

Look at answers A and B.

• Which answer is better?
• What makes it better?

Now look again at the mark scheme on page 35. Find elements of each answer (A and B) that match that mark scheme.

Starting your writing

Your writing needs to:

• communicate clearly, effectively and imaginatively
• use tone, style and register that are appropriate for the given form, purpose and audience.

If you engage your reader effectively and in an appropriate way at the start of the writing, then the exam marker will have immediate confidence in you.

Look back at the 'personal challenge' task in the Work it! on page 40. How might you begin your description? Look at these different opening paragraphs about a personal challenge:

WORKIT!

Student answer A

I am going to write about my thoughts and feelings as I faced the personal challenge of joining a new school. The first thought I had was that if I messed it up in the first few moments, it would live with me forever. I went to reception.

Student answer B

As I stood watching the whirling children, I knew that the first introductions would shape the rest of my days in this school. Thoughts scattering with dread, I slowly opened the gate and walked into reception. My heart pounded.

Here is what an exam marker wrote about each answer:

Student answer A

This answer is working at a low Band 2. It is mainly clear in expression and some words are chosen with care (for example, 'it would live with me forever'). However, the content does not match the purpose of a piece of descriptive writing at the start ('I am going to write about my thoughts and feelings as I faced the personal challenge of joining a new school').

Student answer B

This answer is working at Band 4. It is convincing and compelling and assuredly matches register to purpose, form and audience. There is evidence of wide vocabulary – for example, 'scattering with dread'.

One common trap that students fall into when writing descriptions is to use incomplete sentences. This is especially true when students just copy phrases from their plans straight into their writing. It is as though the student is writing a series of captions for a scene rather than a proper description. Here are some incomplete sentences (captions) that could go with the castle picture you have already worked with:

- Squatting on the lake
- Sandy brown in the mid-afternoon light
- An access bridge like an outstretched tongue

Here is the first incomplete sentence turned into a full sentence:

The castle squats on the lake.

Sometimes incomplete sentences can be joined together into one flowing sentence. For example:

Sandy brown in the mid-afternoon light, the castle squats on the lake with its access bridge stretched out like a tongue.

DO IT!

Turn the other two incomplete sentences into full sentences.

Look at an extract from a student's writing about a frosty morning:

> Snow and ice everywhere on the paths and roads. People's footsteps showing the route they had taken, engraved deep and easy to see. Frost on the branches slowly turning to ice as another layer started to grow.

Now look at the corrected extract below:

> Snow and ice are everywhere on the paths and roads. People's footsteps are showing the routes they have taken and are engraved deep and easy to see. Frost on the branches is slowly turning to ice as another layer starts to grow.

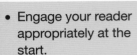

NAILIT!

- Engage your reader appropriately at the start.
- Use your plan and your annotations.
- Use the mark scheme to make sure your writing is as sophisticated as it can be.
- Avoid incomplete sentences.

CHECKIT! ✓

1 What is meant by 'annotating the question'?

2 What is involved in planning an answer?

3 What is important about the opening of your writing?

4 Which is the better opening below, and why?

   a Cradled in the blue-green waters of the Indian Ocean, the beach shimmers gently like a dream of paradise.

   b The sea is a sort of bluey-green, and the beach is lovely and bright and hot. It is just perfect for me.

5 Which of the following are incomplete sentences?

   a The sky grazed the white-capped waves at the horizon.

   b My heart thumped with nerves.

   c Heart thumping with nerves.

   d Next to the bacon was the shiniest, roundest fried egg I'd ever seen.

   e The plumpest sausage I'd ever tasted.

Question type 3: narrative writing with a visual stimulus

Here is an example of a narrative writing with a visual stimulus task:

A local travel agent is planning a display of story openings with beach settings. Your English teacher has asked you to write for the display.

Write a story suggested by this picture:

[40 marks]

NAIL IT!

Remember, even if you are not taking an Edexcel or AQA exam, you will find some more useful advice in this section about writing effectively in the exam.

Preparation and planning

You should approach writing a story based on a picture in the same way that you would approach any other narrative writing:

- plan your ideas and some of the language you will use
- engage your reader at the start of your writing
- don't forget the mark scheme.

Writing tasks will ask you to only base your writing on the picture. It should therefore be a platform, a starting point, for your own ideas.

When answering this type of question you should:

- make notes around the picture stimulus
- ask yourself questions in your notes
- think in terms of narrative events rather than just describing what is there
- use the picture as a starting point: literally think outside the box.

Spend a few minutes studying the picture and asking yourself questions about it.

Below are the notes that one student made on the picture.

WORKIT!

Perhaps they are all watching something happening at sea? Perhaps a fleet of speed boats is approaching the beach?

What is just outside the picture on this side? What if it is high fences and armed guards? Perhaps this is a beach being guarded from terrorist attack.

The picture is taken from a high angle. Is someone watching the beach through binoculars, perhaps on a hotel balcony?

Perhaps someone has just realised that he cannot see his wife and one of his children. Lost? Kidnapped? Running away from him?

What is interesting about this student's notes is that they are definitely seeing the picture as a source for a story, not a description. That is important: a picture stimulus for a story risks getting purely descriptive responses from students.

Here is the opening of a student's writing about the beach picture:

WORKIT!

From his observation tower on the promenade, Marcus scoured the beach with his binoculars. In his dark grey, ill-fitting uniform, he felt uncomfortable under the merciless midday sun. His watch bleeped the fifteen-minute signal, and he briefly lowered his binoculars to give the compulsory 'all ok' wave to his comrades in the neighbouring towers. 'Don't ignore the bleep,' their fat, useless commander always warned them. 'It's the bleep of life. Dead men ignore the bleep.' Marcus raised the glasses again, and sweat mingled with a rising sense of resentment as his magnified gaze swept across the lucky bodies on the beach.

> Suddenly, his attention was caught by two details: firstly, a sunburnt man standing on tip-toe, shading his eyes and peering into the distance, and then – almost immediately afterwards – a roaring sound that grew louder with every second. He swung his binoculars in the direction of this noise and was alarmed to see a whole fleet of large speed boats racing towards the shore, their prows raised on waves of white froth.

DO IT!

Compare this writing with the descriptors in the mark scheme on page 35.

Notice how this student has used their notes on the picture. Notice too how they have tried to use two typical elements of narrative fiction: action and character. This has helped them to avoid writing purely descriptively.

This writing is firmly in the top band of the mark scheme: Band 4. This is what one exam marker said about this student's writing:

> This is a compelling opening that immediately creates a very believable character in Marcus: we seem to get to know him straight away. We assume he is some sort of security guard but the low-quality, impractical uniform hints that he works for a company that is not very professional. This impression is confirmed by the description of the 'commander'. The student uses ambitious and creative vocabulary to keep the atmosphere alive: 'magnified gaze', 'scoured' and 'merciless'. On the other hand, the student also uses simple language choices when he wants to speed up the action. Although the writing is in the third person – 'he', 'Marcus' – we get the sense that we are getting Marcus' view of events and this helps the reader to sympathise with Marcus.

DO IT!

Find a variety of interesting pictures. Make notes around each picture. Think beyond the frame of the picture.

CHECK IT!

1 What does 'thinking outside the box' mean for picture stimulus questions?

2 Action is one main element of narrative fiction that makes it different from description. Name one other element.

Question type 4: narrative writing – the opening to a story

Here is an example of a narrative writing – the opening to a story task:

> You are going to enter a creative writing competition.
>
> Your entry will be judged by a panel of people of your own age.
>
> Write the opening part of a story about a place that has been damaged by a storm.
>
> **[40 marks]**

Preparation and planning

Your plan will help you to write a developed, coherent narrative. The opening is crucial. The first few lines of your writing will let the marker know if your writing is going to be appropriate and engaging, so it is worth practising some methods of getting your reader's interest right at the start.

Narrative hooks

It is possible to put story or novel openings into categories. These are often called **narrative hooks**. When you are generating your story ideas, it is helpful to know some of these categories or types of narrative hooks.

NAILIT!

The section on narrative hooks applies to question type 5 too.

Type of hook	Example
The hook that sets the mood and atmosphere	We started dying before the snow, and like the snow, we continued to fall. Louise Erdrich, *Tracks* (1988)
The hook that causes the reader to raise questions or surprises the reader	It was a pleasure to burn. Ray Bradbury, *Fahrenheit 451* (1953)
	It was the day my grandmother exploded. Iain Banks, *The Crow Road* (1992)
The hook that focuses on a character	In my younger and more vulnerable years my father gave me some advice that I've been turning over in my mind ever since. F Scott Fitzgerald, *The Great Gatsby* (1925)
The hook that starts with a key event or action	It was a wrong number that started it, the telephone ringing three times in the dead of night, and the voice on the other end asking for someone he was not. Paul Auster, *City of Glass* (1985)
The hook which addresses the reader directly	You don't know about me without you have read a book by the name of *The Adventures of Tom Sawyer*; but that ain't no matter. Mark Twain, *Adventures of Huckleberry Finn* (1885)
The hook that begins with dialogue	'Take my camel, dear,' said my Aunt Dot, as she climbed down from this animal on her return from High Mass. Rose Macaulay, *The Towers of Trebizond* (1956)
The hook that describes the setting	In the late summer of that year we lived in a house in a village that looked across the river and the plain to the mountains. Ernest Hemingway, *A Farewell to Arms* (1929)

Here are the first few lines of the novel *Never Let Me Go* by Kazuo Ishiguro and some thoughts by a student who had not read the rest of the book:

WORKIT!

Very direct opening. It sounds like she is talking to me.

Not really descriptive – more factual.

'waste of space' is unusually informal for a narrative. That sort of language is usually only used in speech in stories.

"My name is Kathy H. I'm thirty-one years old, and I've been a carer now for over eleven years. That sounds long enough, I know, but actually they want me to go on for another eight months, until the end of this year. That'll make it almost exactly twelve years. Now I know my being a carer so long isn't necessarily because they think I'm fantastic at what I do. There are some really good carers who've been told to stop after just two or three years. And I can think of one carer at least who went on for all of fourteen years despite being a complete waste of space. So I'm not trying to boast. But then I do know for a fact they've been pleased with my work, and by and large, I have too. My donors have always tended to do much better than expected. Their recovery times have been impressive, and hardly any of them have been classified as 'agitated,' even before fourth donation."

The style sounds more like talking than writing. I feel like I know Kathy and we're having a conversation.

I feel uneasy now: why would a donor not be expected to do well? Why would anyone be a repeat donor? What would they be donating? She's a carer so they must be donating body parts!

DOIT!

1 Find seven different novels or stories written for adults. Try not to spend too long thinking about your choices. A good way of doing this activity is to go to your school library or local library fiction section and simply take seven novels off the shelves at random.
Read the first page of each novel in turn. Don't turn the first page – even if the page stops in mid-sentence. Now answer these questions:

- How is the writer trying to hook me into the story?
- Does the first page have characters, descriptions, dialogue?
- What sort of story is this? (Horror? Real-life drama? Romance?)
- What will happen in the story?
- What clues on the first page suggest what might happen?

2 Do the same exercise for the first page of a modern novel you have studied on your GCSE course. Try to forget that you have read the whole novel. Try to re-read the first page 'for the first time'.

3 Find another novel. Turn straight to the second page. Read up to page ten or to the end of the chapter – whichever comes first. Now try to write the 'missing' first page. Finally, compare your version with the real first page.

DO IT!

1 Look at the three openings below written by students. Decide which narrative hook each student has used.

Student answer A

The sea surged against the rocks as the storm continued its war on the village. Gates swung from hinges that could barely hold on. In Devon this was nothing new, but the villagers were still afraid.

Student answer B

I need to tell you something right from the start. Storms are different here. You think you have seen it all on the Geographic channel? You're wrong.

Student answer C

'Move away from that window!' she screamed as the torrent of water simultaneously flooded through the door and the windows. The baby woke and began to wail as chaos swirled in with the water.

2 Which do you think is most successful?

3 Try out three different types of hook for your opening to a story about a place that is damaged by a storm.

4 Write three or four sentences for each type of hook listed in the table on page 48.

DO IT!

Describe each of the events below to show what is happening, rather than telling your reader what is happening.

- A man got his car stuck in mud. He was angry.
- A boy fell over and cut his hand.
- The dog was excited by the snow.

Show don't tell

When you are writing either a narrative (story) or a description, it is important to **show** your reader details rather than to **tell** them. For example, if your character is cold in your story, it is better to show that they are cold by the way they speak and behave rather than just to tell your reader 'they were cold'. Look at the example below:

Tell	Show
She was cold	Shoulders hunched against the wind, she pushed her hands further into her coat pockets. Her scarf whipped against her face as she moved stubbornly down the street.

CHECK IT! ✓

1 Seven different narrative hooks have been explained in this section. Each of the openings below uses at least one of these seven hooks. Which hooks are used by each opening?

a She caught a glimpse of the hotel through the fading light. It shone like a jewel. She crouched into the cover of the thick undergrowth and stealthily made her way towards her target. It was certainly a perfect, tranquil place, but no guest would get much sleep that night.

b When she had finally finished swimming, she carefully put her leg back on.

c You know how it's always just when you're about to do something that your parents ask you if you've done it yet? Well, that's what makes me mad.

2 Rewrite the following sentence so that it shows, rather than tells: *He was clumsy.*

3 Name five things you should try to include in the first page of your story in order to engage the reader.

Question type 5: narrative writing – a complete story

A typical narrative question for the exam paper could be:

> You have been invited to produce a piece of creative writing for a local newspaper.
>
> Write a story about a celebration or party that goes badly wrong.
>
> **[40 marks]**

Preparation and planning

You are writing a whole story, so you need to keep the plot manageable. You also need to make sure that the story is believable.

- Keep your storyline simple – the events, characters and settings only matter if you portray them in exciting ways.

- You are better opting for an exciting 'single-event story' with one or two characters and telling it well, rather than planning a complicated story and running out of time.

- Keep your storyline simple by keeping to personal experience. You will write more convincingly about situations you know or understand.

- Use a simple structure to help you shape your ideas. Here is a simple four-part structure that can be used in a story you will have a short while to plan and write:

  1. Normality
  2. Disruption/problem
  3. Climax/crisis
  4. Return to normality/result

- Never use clichéd endings '... and then I woke up and it was all a dream...' '... and they lived happily ever after.'

- Don't over-use dialogue, as this can get out of control and make your writing difficult to follow.

Look at the table on page 52, showing a four-part structure for creative writing. It is an example of a student's planning notes for a story about a celebration or party that goes badly wrong.

NAILIT!

For this type of question, you will be asked to write a **whole** story, whereas in the fourth question type (on page 48) you will be asked to write only **the opening** to a story.

DOIT!

Using the plan in the table, write the opening paragraph to this story.

WORKIT!

Normality	1st person narrative
	Going to an 18th birthday party
	Lots of fun and noise
Disruption/problem	Lots of dancing and drinking
	Everyone having lots of fun, but risks are becoming clear (drunkenness)
Climax/crisis	Someone suggests setting off the fireworks
	Description of the fireworks
	One firework doesn't go off... disaster
Return to normality/result	After the party in hospital
	A new version of normality

Here is one student's writing using the plan:

WORKIT!

Everyone said you should never return. Why didn't I listen?

It was the 18th birthday of the year and the focal party for our group where we all thought about reaching adulthood. We had started the evening by ordering takeaway, and as I phoned the order through, Chris got the party started.

'Food shouldn't be long,' I said as we walked into the living room to just give it one last check.

After months of planning, we had everything we needed to host the perfect party. We had food. We had drink and we had entertainment. By planning down to the last detail, we knew we had thought of everything. The music was good and loud. We had researched loads of drinking games and best of all – we had fireworks.

As people arrived and the atmosphere livened up, the drink went down faster and faster.

Everybody was dancing round and Chris skittered past me, wearing a badge saying '18 today'. As I made my way through the living room, my feet were unsteady beneath me. I realised that I'd had too much to drink. Chris and Mel were in the corner, drinking shots of vodka one after the other. The bottle was almost empty. 'Time for the fireworks?' he asked.

'I think so,' I agreed.

We picked up the bag of fireworks from the kitchen where we had left it, and made our way up the garden path. The night was cold and dark and the only noise to be heard was the music coming from the house. As we lit the first fuse, a glowing orange rocket shot upward, exploding into a flower of silver and blue crackles.

People crowded by the door to see. Cheers and whoops of joy surrounded us. One by one the rockets set off, until we came to the very last one – the big one.

As I lit the fuse I was full of anticipation, waiting to be amazed by a huge display of sounds and sights – but they didn't come. I looked back at the fuse. It wasn't lit. Everyone said you should never go back, but I didn't listen. Unsteadily I bent down towards the fuse...

I lay in bed, and touched my face. I felt a bandage and in my heart I knew that I should have listened. Everyone said you should never return.

DO IT!

1 Try to apply the four-part story structure to this story. Find the points where each of the four parts begins.
2 Use the mark scheme on page 35 to assess this student's writing.
 a Decide on the band.
 b Find three descriptors from the mark scheme to support why you have placed the writing in that band.

✓ CHECK IT!

1 Why is personal experience often good material for a story in the exam?
2 What four-part structure could be used for a story?
3 Name two things that can ruin a story.

Fiction: Writing

1 How many creative writing tasks will be offered in the exam?

2 Which sorts of writing might you have to choose from in this writing exam?

3 What percentage of the marks for the writing task are given to VSSSP?

4 Name three typical features of narrative.

5 How much time should you leave for the fiction writing section?

6 How much time should you spend planning the writing task?

7 Name three types of figurative language.

8 What metaphor has been extended in the following text?

> Sally glanced back at her pursuer, who kept closing the gap, never deviating from the invisible track he seemed to be gliding along. His face had a metallic gleam in the sunlight and the pistons of his arms and legs never faltered for a moment.

9 Name a trap to avoid when doing descriptive writing.

10 For which sort of writing task is 'before, during and after' a useful planning structure?

11 Which of the following sentences is incomplete?

   a A delicious aroma of chocolate.   b As I had promised to do it, I did.   c She ran.

12 What is the most important thing to remember about the opening of a story?

13 Name three common narrative hooks that can be used at the start of a story.

14 What is the difference between showing and telling?

15 Rewrite this sentence so that it shows rather than tells:

She was selfish.

16 Name a simple four-phase story structure that you could use in the exam.

17 You have been invited to produce a piece of creative writing about fears and superstitions.

Write a story set in or near a deserted house. AO5 AO6

Non-fiction: Reading

Introduction and advice

In the reading section of the non-fiction paper, you will be given two non-fiction texts on a similar topic. There will be questions on each of the texts and questions that ask you to compare them. Some questions will ask you simply to find information in the texts, but the main focus of this section is on how writers try to influence readers and make them respond in particular ways.

You will be tested against the following assessment objectives for reading:

	• Identify and interpret explicit and implicit information and ideas. • Select and synthesise evidence from different texts.
	Explain, comment on and analyse how writers use language and structure to achieve effects and influence readers, using relevant subject terminology to support their views.
	Compare writers' ideas and perspectives, as well as how these are conveyed, across two or more texts.
	Evaluate texts critically and support this with appropriate textual references.

NAILIT!

- First, spend at least 15 minutes reading the questions, then the texts. Make notes as you read.

- Next, spend at least 45 minutes writing the answers.

- Leave time to check and change your answers at the end.

Differences between the exam boards

SNAPIT! **Personalise it! Non-fiction: Reading**

Board	
AQA	☞ One of the two texts will have been written before 1900. ☞ There will be four questions to answer. Questions 1 and 2 assess AO1, Question 3 assesses AO2 and Question 4 assesses AO3. ☞ The section is worth 40 marks. ☞ You should spend 1 hour on this section.
Edexcel	☞ Both texts will have been written after 1900. There will be seven questions to answer. Questions 1, 4 and 7a assess AO1. Questions 2, 3 and 5 assess AO2, Question 7b assesses AO3 and Question 6 assesses AO4. ☞ The section is worth 56 marks. ☞ You should spend 1 hour 15 minutes on this section.
Eduqas	☞ One of the two texts will have been written before 1900. ☞ There will be six questions to answer. Questions 1, 3 and 5 assess AO1, Question 2 assesses AO2, Question 6 assesses AO3 and Question 4 assesses AO4. ☞ The section is worth 40 marks. ☞ You should spend 1 hour on this section.
OCR	☞ Paper 1 focuses on non-fiction (it is Paper 2 for the other boards). ☞ There will be two extracts from different texts, and one of these might be literary non-fiction, such as an autobiography or travel writing. One of the two texts will have been written before 1900. ☞ There will be four questions to answer. Questions 1 and 2 assess AO1, Question 3 assesses AO2 and Question 4 assesses AO3 and AO4. ☞ The section is worth 40 marks. ☞ You should spend 1 hour on this section.

AO1: Identifying and interpreting information and ideas

Assessment objective 1 tests your ability to identify information and ideas in a text.

Identifying facts and other explicit details in the text

Some of the questions on the non-fiction reading paper – especially the first question – will test whether you can find the explicit information that is actually there in front of you. For example:

> Read the newspaper article, 'Food for Thought'.
>
> (a) Name one food that Jennifer Thompson says is bad for us.
>
> (b) Name one chef Jennifer Thompson says has made healthy food more appealing.
>
> (c) Give one reason, according to the writer, why many people prefer food that is bad for them.

NAILIT!

Read information questions carefully and answer them accurately.

If you are sitting the AQA exam you will be given statements that are true and statements that are false in Question 1 of the non-fiction reading section of the exam.

You need to read carefully and accurately to make sure you have understood the ideas and information that the writer is giving you. The exam markers expect you to find 'true statements' from the extract. Remember that the statements may sound true – or may be true to you, but you need to **focus on what is in the extract**.

Inference: reading between the lines

Implied information is not directly there in front of us: we have to infer it. Some questions will require you to infer a piece of information. For example, in the Work it! on the following page we **know** that statement A is correct because the writer uses the exact words in the suggested statement: 'I try to block it out.' For statement B, though, we have to infer that when the writer says that parents are 'being driven slowly insane' this **must** mean that they dislike the song, although the writer does not literally say that.

NAILIT!

Sometimes you have to work out (infer) information you have been asked for. Inferring means reading between the lines.

WORKIT!

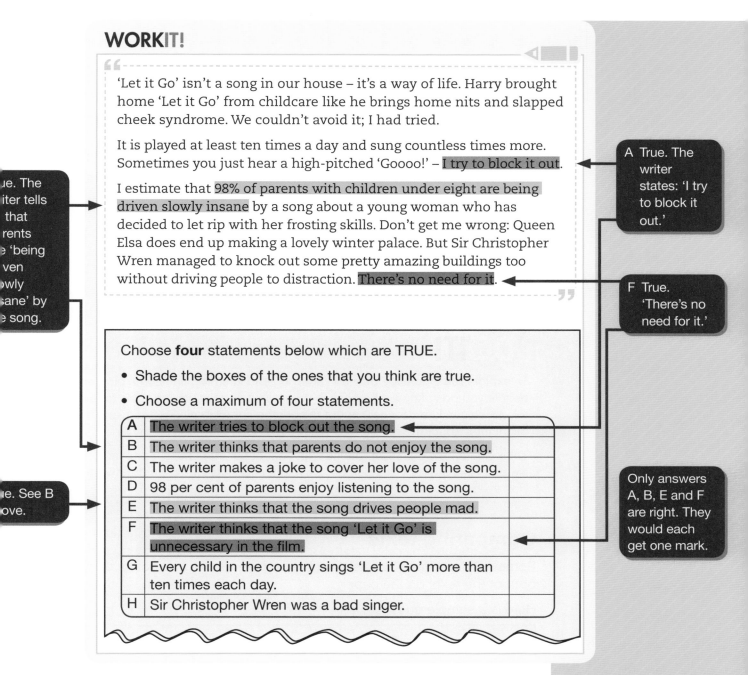

'Let it Go' isn't a song in our house – it's a way of life. Harry brought home 'Let it Go' from childcare like he brings home nits and slapped cheek syndrome. We couldn't avoid it; I had tried.

It is played at least ten times a day and sung countless times more. Sometimes you just hear a high-pitched 'Goooo!' – I try to block it out.

I estimate that 98% of parents with children under eight are being driven slowly insane by a song about a young woman who has decided to let rip with her frosting skills. Don't get me wrong: Queen Elsa does end up making a lovely winter palace. But Sir Christopher Wren managed to knock out some pretty amazing buildings too without driving people to distraction. There's no need for it.

A True. The writer states: 'I try to block it out.'

F True. 'There's no need for it.'

ue. The iter tells that rents e 'being ven wly ane' by song.

ue. See B ove.

Choose **four** statements below which are TRUE.

• Shade the boxes of the ones that you think are true.

• Choose a maximum of four statements.

A	The writer tries to block out the song.
B	The writer thinks that parents do not enjoy the song.
C	The writer makes a joke to cover her love of the song.
D	98 per cent of parents enjoy listening to the song.
E	The writer thinks that the song drives people mad.
F	The writer thinks that the song 'Let it Go' is unnecessary in the film.
G	Every child in the country sings 'Let it Go' more than ten times each day.
H	Sir Christopher Wren was a bad singer.

Only answers A, B, E and F are right. They would each get one mark.

DOIT!

1 Look again at the correct statements E and F. Explain whether each of these is literally true, or whether we have to infer that they are true.
2 List five things from your everyday life that you know are true but only because you infer it.

Interpreting implicit information

We need to look more carefully at this idea of implied – or implicit – information. Sometimes a writer lets us know something without telling us directly.

Here is a sentence from a text:

> " Crocodiles can swim under water, and if that crocodile had wanted to eat the diver, the boat would not have been able to prevent it. "

If you are asked what we learn here about crocodiles, we learn that:

- crocodiles can swim under water (factual detail)

- the boat wouldn't have stopped a crocodile attack (factual detail)

- the crocodile did not choose to attack at that moment (inference).

DO IT!

To explore the difference between knowing and inferring, find some pictures of people you don't know – perhaps in magazines or newspapers – and jot down things we can know (or see) about the person (for example, gender), and things we might infer about them from their picture (perhaps they look angry).

Think about how our assumptions might affect our inferences. For example, if we don't like the look of a person, we might infer that they are untrustworthy. However, we could be wrong.

Comparing texts

Some AO1 questions will ask you to compare details and points of view in both of the texts on the paper.

Here is a sample question:

> Using information from both texts explain how attitudes to healthy eating have changed over time.

You should take a four-step approach to comparison questions:

1. Underline the focus for the question to make sure you keep on track.

2. Find details in the texts relating to these key words. Underline and annotate the texts.

3. As you work, ask yourself, 'What can I work out (infer) from this relevant detail?'

4. Bring relevant details and inferences from both texts together in your own answer.

NAIL IT!

AQA Question 2 will ask you to compare both sources and write a summary. Here, 'summary' just means concentrating on the essential information being asked for, and putting it into your own words (with brief quotations to support your points).

NAIL IT!

All the information you need will be in the two texts: you are not expected to use your own knowledge.

You can write your answer to comparison questions in two ways:

1. Write about both sources at once by merging your ideas into one paragraph.

2. Write two linked paragraphs where you talk about each source in turn, using comparing (and/or contrasting) words to make links as you go (for example, 'however' and 'similarly'). These words are sometimes called discourse markers or connectives.

DO IT!

Make a list of words and phrases that could help you to interpret, compare and contrast in this question.

Mark scheme for identifying and interpreting information and ideas (AO1)

SNAPIT!

Mark scheme level	Band 2 descriptors (Roughly GCSE grades 2–3)	Band 3 descriptors (Roughly GCSE grades 4–6)	Band 4 descriptors (Roughly GCSE grades 7–9)
The student's answer...	• interprets • tries to infer • chooses some appropriate detail.	• clearly synthesises and interprets • makes clear inferences • chooses clear, relevant details.	• perceptively synthesises and interprets • makes perceptive inferences • chooses very precise, relevant details.
Comparison questions	• refers to at least one of the texts • points out some relevant similarities and/or difference(s).	• refers to both texts • points out clear, relevant similarities and/or differences between texts.	• refers to both texts • explores perceptive, relevant similarities and/or differences between texts.

✓ CHECKIT!

1. What are the most important things to keep in mind about AO1 non-fiction questions? Write them down.

2. Read this extract:

> I suppose it's understandable that 'Let It Go' is so popular. It's a tune about a moody adolescent yet it appeals strongly to very young children. Perhaps it's proof that kids are getting genetically stroppier earlier. As far as I can remember it's the first time pre-schoolers have adopted their own anthem with such passion. Either way it's a fantastic introduction to the world of pop where you can be in love with someone on Monday, spend too much time listening to them on Tuesday, and loathe them by Wednesday.

Write four things we learn from this text.

NAILIT!

All the exam boards test AO2 with a higher-tariff question in the non-fiction reading section, so a lengthy answer is needed. Edexcel also assess AO2 with two low-mark questions.

AO2: How writers use language and structure to influence readers

AO2 questions in the non-fiction reading section of the exam will test your understanding of how one of the writers uses language and structure to put their ideas across to the reader, and to engage or influence them. In other words, the questions will be about a writer's choices and their impact on the reader. You will be expected to use appropriate subject terminology and quotations to support your points.

The key focuses for AO2 questions are:

SNAPIT!

Key focus	Explanation
Words	You need to think about the words – the vocabulary – the writer has chosen. All of us express things in different ways: we make choices. We choose our words carefully so that we use the right ones for the effect we want to have. Writers choose very carefully. Sometimes paying attention to individual words can be revealing for a reader.
Phrases	When words are joined into phrases, sometimes the phrase is more powerful than the individual words. Look at how words are combined for effect.
Language features and techniques	These are specific devices used by the writer: such as, similes, metaphors, rhetorical questions, and so on. Never just spot these devices: write about their effect on the reader.
Sentence forms	Writers can say the same thing in different ways to different effects. They achieve this partly by varying the lengths of sentences and the order of information in them. Look out for sentence variety.
Structural features	See page 18 and the Glossary for detailed information on structure. **(Not AQA)**
Effect (and tone)	This is about how the reader responds to the writer's words: what does it make them think of? How does it make them feel? The tone of the writing is the writer's attitude and their viewpoint. They could, for example, be sarcastic, passionate, dignified, mocking or polite.
Your views	These are your beliefs about what the writer is trying to do and how they are trying to do it.
Evidence	These are the details from the text that you choose in order to support the views you put forward. Evidence can be in the form of quotations, especially in this answer.
Subject terminology	These are technical words about language. English subject terminology includes words and phrases like sentence, verb, simile, rhetorical question.

NAILIT!

AQA is the only board that will not ask you about structure in the non-fiction paper.

Below is a short extract from a letter to the President of the United States in 1852. It is not certain who wrote the letter, but many believe the author was Chief Seattle, a Native American leader.

> The President in Washington sends word that he wishes to buy our land. But how can you buy or sell the sky? The land? The idea is strange to us. If we do not own the freshness of the air and the sparkle of the water, how can you sell them? Every part of this earth is sacred to my people. Every shining pine needle, every humming insect. All are holy in the memory and experience of my people. We know the sap which courses through the trees as we know the blood that courses through our veins. We are part of the earth and it is part of us. The perfumed flowers are our sisters. The bear, the deer, the great eagle, these are our brothers. The rocky crests, the juices in the meadow, the body heat of a pony, and man, all belong to the same family. The shining water that moves in the streams and rivers is not just water, but the blood of our ancestors. If we sell you our land, you must remember that it is sacred. Each ghostly reflection in the clear waters of the lakes tells of events and memories in the life of my people. The waters murmur in the voice of my father's father. The rivers are our brothers. They quench our thirst. They carry our canoes and feed our children. So you must give to the river the kindness you would give any brother.

A typical question using this text would be:

> How does Chief Seattle try to influence the President of the United States?

Firstly, think about the purpose of the text and its audience. What is written in this letter – the content – should match the purpose (why it was written) and the audience (the intended reader).

Read part of a student's answer, dealing with the purpose and audience of the extract:

WORKIT!

The purpose of this text is to influence the thinking of the President of America. Chief Seattle is responding to a request to buy land. His first purpose is to challenge the president's thinking about the land and this request. He begins by posing questions 'how can you buy or sell the sky? The land?' Within our society we understand the concept of selling land. However, the idea of selling the sky is as 'strange' to us as it is to Chief Seattle. The word 'strange' has the effect of challenging and surprising the reader – as it would also challenge the President of the United States. The tone is formal and measured. It does not attack but by raising these seemingly simple questions he challenges what we understand by ownership of the land.

View and evidence.

Subject terminology.

Analyse the effect of the writer's choice of language.

NAILIT!

Texts used in the exam are likely to be longer than this.

DOIT!

Now, let's look carefully at the effect of language. Read the short extract from Chief Seattle's letter again (page 61). Look very carefully at references to family. To help us answer the example question on page 61, we could consider how Chief Seattle uses references to family to influence the president.

1 Write up to six lines about how Chief Seattle uses references to family to influence the president, using the three rules in the Nail it! below.
2 When you have written your answer, compare it with the two below from the other students. Decide which of the three answers is best, and why.
3 Think about which answer makes best use of the three rules.
4 Find examples of those rules being used in the two answers below **and** the answer in the Work it! on page 61.

NAILIT!

Make sure you stick to these rules:

- Explain your views, and use some evidence.
- Use some subject terminology.
- Analyse the effect of the writer's choice of language.

WORKIT!

Student answer A

Chief Seattle uses references to family to show that we are 'part of the earth' just like family. He uses lists to show that there are lots of things that we are part of.

Student answer B

Chief Seattle links the 'sap' that courses through trees with the 'blood' that runs through our veins. This metaphor of life-blood is linked to the idea of family blood lines. To Chief Seattle, all living things are connected to the earth. He lists different elements of the planet – 'the bear, the deer, the great eagle' – as well as listing family links: 'brother', 'grandfather'. The effect of this listing makes it sound like a prayer. This effect links to the 'sacred' earth that contains the blood of his ancestors.

Mark scheme for language and structure (AO2)

SNAPIT! Mark scheme for language and structure (AO2)

Mark scheme level	Band 2 descriptors (Roughly GCSE grades 2–3)	Band 3 descriptors (Roughly GCSE grades 4–6)	Band 4 descriptors (Roughly GCSE grades 7–9)
The student's answer...	• makes some simple, relevant comments • shows some understanding of how language and structure are used for effects, and to influence • uses some appropriate textual detail • makes some use of subject terminology, mainly appropriately.	• makes accurate comments • begins to analyse how language and structure are used for effects, and to influence • uses a range of relevant textual detail • makes accurate use of subject terminology to support points effectively.	• makes perceptive comments • gives a detailed, perceptive analysis of how language and structure are used for effects, and to influence • uses a range of precisely chosen textual detail • makes sophisticated and accurate use of subject terminology to support points effectively.

Here is student answer B with some marker's comments in the margin:

WORKIT!

Chief Seattle links the 'sap' that courses through trees with the 'blood' that runs through our veins. This metaphor of life-blood is linked to the idea of family blood lines. To Chief Seattle, all living things are connected to the earth. He lists different elements of the planet – 'the bear, the deer, the great eagle' – as well as listing family links: 'brother', 'grandfather'. The effect of this listing makes it sound like a prayer. This effect links to the 'sacred' earth that contains the blood of his ancestors.

> Makes some use of subject terminology, mainly appropriately. Although this isn't strictly a metaphor, it makes a useful comparison between 'sap' and 'blood'.

> Shows detailed and perceptive understanding of language.

> Uses a range of relevant textual detail.

This snippet from an answer is strong in some places, weaker in others.

DOIT!

1 Look carefully through your own answer (that you wrote for the Do it! on page 62). Find examples of descriptors from the mark scheme in your answer. Compare the mark scheme with student answer A on page 62.
2 Reconsider your rank order for student answers A and B, and the answer in the Work it! on page 61.

NAILIT!

Language and structure questions will focus on one text.

✓ CHECKIT!

1 What are the most important things to keep in mind about AO2 questions? Write them down.

2 What does the language and structure question focus on?

3 In his letter to the president, Chief Seattle uses rhetorical questions. Write down at least two other specific language techniques that he uses. Give examples.

4 What are the effects of these techniques on the reader?

AO3: Comparing writers' ideas and perspectives

☞ AQA assess AO3 in Question 4. It is worth 16 marks.

☞ Edexcel assess AO3 in Question 7b. It is worth 14 marks.

☞ Eduqas assess AO3 in Question 6. It is worth 10 marks.

☞ OCR assess AO3 in Question 4. Question 4 also assesses AO4. The total marks for the question is 18 – there are 6 marks for AO3.

AO3 assesses your ability to compare writers' ideas and perspectives (their points of view), and how they use language to convey their ideas. Here are two examples of AO3 questions:

> Both of these texts are about food and health.
>
> Compare:
>
> (a) how the writers feel about food and health
>
> (b) how they make their views clear to the reader.
>
> **OR**
>
> Compare how the writers of these texts present their ideas and perspectives about food and health.

AO3 questions will tend to mention the writers. You need to show your understanding of **what** you have read in both texts and **how** the texts are written in order to convey the writers' attitudes, points of view or perspectives.

The key focuses for AO3 questions are:

 # SNAPIT!

Key word	Meaning
Compare	The word 'compare' asks you to identify and analyse the main similarities and differences between the texts. Remember the texts will have been carefully selected to allow you to be able to do this.
Methods	The word 'method' asks you to write about form, structure and language. • Form is the format or text type, such as a letter, diary, article, etc. • Structure is the way the content and ideas are organised. • Language is the choice of words that the writer has chosen to use. It is 'how' a writer creates the text.
Convey	The word 'convey' in the question literally means to 'communicate' or 'send'. In the exam it means that you must write about the effects of the language used as well as tone, imagery, emphasis or bias. It's important to think about what we are told in each text and what has been left out.
Support	The use of the word 'support' here means that you must use quotations, from both texts, to act as evidence for your points.
Ideas and perspectives	These are the writers' thoughts, viewpoints, impressions and attitudes.

For this question it is also important to remember that exam markers are looking for **detailed** responses – you must make sure that you write enough. This question carries a high number of marks and so it will need a longer, more developed answer.

You can **interweave** your ideas from both texts, or write about each text, making occasional relevant comparisons.

We are going to compare two texts from cookery books. The first text is from *The Book of Household Management* which appeared in 1861 and was written by Mrs Beeton. The second text is by Nigella Lawson, a popular cook, journalist and TV personality. The text appeared on her website.

Read the titles of the two texts. Notice the tone of each of them and the differences in the language used.

> BOILED CAULIFLOWERS
>
> Mrs Beeton

> Warm spiced cauliflower and chickpea salad with pomegranate seeds
>
> Nigella Lawson

Read one student's notes in response to these titles:

WORKIT!

Mrs Beeton

We know the key ingredient - cauliflower - but we don't know anything else.

The adjective 'boiled' provides a straightforward description of what will be happening to the cauliflower.

The word 'boiled' sounds plain and not very comforting.

The tone is practical - no nonsense.

Nigella Lawson

We are given almost a complete list of the ingredients.

The adjective 'Warm' makes us think of comfort and 'spiced' makes us think of exotic locations. This also links to 'chickpea' and 'pomegranate'.

'Spiced' also suggests warmth.

The tone is sumptuous and comforting.

DO IT!

Look back over the advice about key focuses in questions that compare ideas and perspectives.

1 Without looking at this book, make a list of key words that are likely to be used in this sort of question.
2 Next to each word (or phrase) explain why it is important.
3 You could make these into flashcards to help you to remember them.

DO IT!

1 Look at the student's notes.
   a Which points do you agree with most strongly?
   b Can you improve some of the others?
   c Can you add any further ideas?
2 Write three or four sentences to compare the language used in the titles of the two cookery texts by Mrs Beeton and Nigella Lawson.

NAIL IT!

- Read the question before you read (or re-read) the two texts.
- Compare the writers' different ideas and perspectives.
- Compare the methods they use to convey their ideas and perspectives.
- Support your response with references to both texts.

NAIL IT!

- About 180 words is a good length to aim for when answering these questions, but making precise points supported by evidence is more important.
- Spend on the answer no more than the number of minutes justified by the mark allocation. For example, if the question offers sixteen marks, then aim to plan for a minute and write for 15 minutes.

Here is a sample exam question:

> Compare how the writers of Text 1 and Text 2 present their different ideas and perspectives of how to cook cauliflower.
>
> Compare:
>
> (a) how the writers feel about cauliflower
>
> (b) how they make their ideas and perspectives clear to the reader.

"

Text 1

BOILED CAULIFLOWERS.

INGREDIENTS. – To each ½ gallon of water allow 1 heaped tablespoonful of salt.

Mode. – Choose cauliflowers that are close and white; trim off the decayed outside leaves, and cut the stalk off flat at the bottom. Open the flower a little in places to remove the insects, which generally are found about the stalk, and let the cauliflowers lie in salt and water for an hour previous to dressing them, with their head downwards: this will effectually draw out all the vermin. Then put them into fast-boiling water, with the addition of salt in the above proportion, and let them boil briskly over a good fire, keeping the sauce-pan uncovered. The water should be well skimmed and, when the cauliflowers are tender, take them up with a slice, let them drain, and, if large enough, place them upright in the dish. Serve with plain melted butter, a little of which may be poured over the flower.

Time. – Small cauliflower, 12 to 15 minutes, large one, 20 to 25 minutes, after the water boils.

Average cost, for large cauliflowers, *6d.* each.

Sufficient. – Allow 1 large cauliflower for 3 persons.

"

DO IT!

Make a list of words and phrases that could help you to compare and bring together information from different texts. These words and phrases are sometimes called discourse markers or connectives. For example:

- On the other hand…
- However…
- But…
- In contrast…
- Similarly…
- This seems to suggest…

Text 2

Warm spiced cauliflower and chickpea salad with pomegranate seeds

This is one of my favourite suppers, although there's nothing that says you can't serve this as a vegetable side as part of a more conventional meal. And you could also bolster it further by crumbling in some feta. But for me, it is perfect just as it is: the tomatoes almost ooze into a dressing in the oven, and the cauliflower softens, but not soggily.

And this is also very, very good cold, so if you have some left over, it makes a fabulous packed lunch, or provides instant gratification on those days you have to eat fridgeside, with your coat still on, you're so hungry.

Method

1   Preheat the oven to 220°C /gas mark 7/425°F. Trim the cauliflower and divide into small florets. Pour the oil into a large bowl, add the cinnamon and cumin seeds, and stir or whisk to help the spices disperse. Tip in the prepared cauliflower and toss to coat. Pour the contents of the bowl into a small oven tray (I mostly use a disposable foil baking tray measuring 30 × 20 cm/12 × 8 inches) and place in the oven for 15 minutes. Don't wash out the bowl you've been using just yet.

2   Add the chickpeas to this bowl, and add the harissa, tasting it first to see if you want both tablespoonfuls, and, at the risk of being repetitive, toss to coat. Quarter the tomatoes and add them to the bowl, and shake or stir to mix. When the cauliflower has had its 15 minutes, remove the tray, quickly tip the chickpeas and tomatoes over the cauliflower, and toss to combine before returning to the oven for a further 15 minutes until the cauliflower is tender.

3   When it's ready, remove from the oven and sprinkle the salt over the vegetables, then (and this isn't the last time) toss to combine with half of the pomegranate seeds before dividing between 2 bowls. Divide the parsley leaves – without chopping them – between the 2 bowls and toss to mix. Scatter with the remaining pomegranate seeds.

Look at the question on page 66 again. Always follow any instructions and prompts below the question.

Here the first prompt is: 'Compare how the writers feel about cauliflower'.

Some elements you could consider are:

- their ideas

- the impressions we are given about the subject – how do the writers present it?

- what we are told and what is left out

- the tone

- the purpose of this text – what is most important to the writer?

NAIL IT!

- In the exam, make some quick notes about how each text uses language, form and structure to convey its ideas and perspective on the topic (such as cooking cauliflower).

- Language is the most important aspect of the writer's methods to concentrate on.

- You do not have to make nearly as many comments about form and structure.

NAIL IT!

If you are given prompts in the question, make sure that you use them!

Look at the notes made by a student below:

WORKIT!

Ideas and perspectives

Source A	Source B
Does not say whether this is a side dish or a main dish, 'Allow 1 large cauliflower for 3 persons'.	States clearly that this could be used as a 'side' dish or a main dish.
Gives detailed, step-by-step instructions, 'Choose cauliflowers that are close and white'.	Gives detailed step-by-step instructions, 'Preheat the oven...', but also adds personal details, 'you have to eat fridgeside, with your coat still on, you're so hungry'.
The tone is practical and instructional: 'Allow', 'Choose'. The tone is detached from the reader.	The tone changes. At first the tone is indulgent and comforting, 'And you could also bolster it further', but then becomes more practical and instructional in the method: 'Pour', 'Divide'. The tone is conversational with the reader with some humour 'eat fridgeside'.
We do not know whether the writer likes cauliflower. This information has been left out.	Provides opinions 'But for me, it is perfect just as it is' and 'provides instant gratification'.
The writer seems to favour 'plain' cooking. The cauliflower is cooked whole with nothing added other than 'plain melted butter'.	The writer seems to favour comforting food with lots of 'oil', 'spices' and 'feta'.
The writer seems to see cauliflower as containing lots of insects, which she describes as 'vermin'.	The writer seems to see cauliflower as a 'favourite' providing 'instant gratification'.

Look carefully at how this student's method has allowed her to compare relevant aspects of the texts.

- Could you improve any of her notes?
- See if you can find any more points of comparison.

Look again at the second prompt beneath the exam question:

(b) (compare) how the writers make their ideas and perspectives clear to the reader.

DOIT!

Use the notes here and your own ideas to compare the ideas and perspectives in the two texts. Write at least two detailed paragraphs.

Again, although this is a suggestion, **always** follow that suggestion.

Some elements you could write about here are:

- What is the form of the writing (the text type)?
- How are the ideas organised and presented?
- What are the key features of the language?
- Word choices.
- Sentence structures.

Here are the thoughts that one student had about the texts' language and methods:

WORKIT!

Method	Source A	Source B
Form	The form is a recipe. It gives step-by-step instructions on how to cook cauliflower. At the end of the recipe it gives additional information about cost, 'Average cost, for large cauliflowers, 6d. each', and how many people an average-sized cauliflower would feed.	The form is a recipe. It gives step-by-step instructions on how to cook a dish using cauliflower. However, at the start there is a section where the writer gives her opinion of the dish, 'This is one of my favourite suppers,' and puts herself in the place of the reader, 'you're so hungry'.
Structure	The recipe uses imperatives to begin each instruction. This is what we would expect for a recipe: 'Allow', 'Choose'.	The recipe section also uses imperatives to begin each instruction. Again, this is what we would expect for a recipe: 'Add', 'Remove', 'Divide'.
Language	Some language will surprise the reader as it has negative associations. We are told to remove 'decayed outside leaves'. We need to 'remove the insects', using salt water to 'draw out all the vermin'. These are words that we would not expect to find in a recipe.	Language used is positive. Cauliflower is a 'favourite' and is 'perfect'. Sensual language: 'ooze', 'tender'.

Mark scheme for comparing writers' ideas and perspectives (AO3)

SNAPIT! Mark scheme for comparing writers' ideas and perspectives (AO3)

Mark scheme level	Band 2 descriptors (Roughly GCSE grades 2–3)	Band 3 descriptors (Roughly GCSE grades 4–6)	Band 4 descriptors (Roughly GCSE grades 7–9)
The student's answer...	• gives a straightforward description of some of the main similarities and differences • tries to compare ideas and perspectives • makes some comments on writers' methods • chooses some appropriate textual detail/references from at least one text • identifies some different ideas and perspectives (or tone).	• compares ideas and perspectives in some detail • explains clearly how writers' methods convey ideas and perspectives • selects relevant detail to support from both texts • shows a clear understanding of the different ideas and perspectives in both texts.	• compares ideas and perspectives in a detailed way • analyses how writers' methods convey ideas and perspectives • selects a range of judicious supporting detail from both texts • shows a detailed understanding of the different ideas and perspectives in both texts.

Read the extract from a student's response to the question on page 66 below, then look at the mark scheme for this question:

WORKIT!

Nigella Lawson writes in an informal tone about food, which matches her relaxed and more modern approach to cookery. She talks about cauliflower using positive language telling the reader that the recipe is one of her 'favourites' that provides 'instant gratification'. She also jokes all the way through her recipe about the number of times the ingredients need to be tossed. Mrs Beeton uses a much more formal tone with her choice of language, 'Choose cauliflowers that are close and white', which reflects the language of the time the recipe was written. Mrs Beeton's instructions are easy to understand and seem to be full of plain common sense. Her recipes are simple using only 'water' and 'salt' with the cauliflower. At the end she suggests that it can be served with 'melted butter' but she adds that this should be 'plain'. Nigella Lawson, however, uses very sensual language to describe her dish.

Here are some exam marker's comments on this student's answer.

This extract from an answer indicates that the full response would achieve Band 3. It compares ideas in a clear and relevant way and is starting to explain clearly how the writers' methods are used. This would need to be developed to secure Band 3. It selects relevant detail from both texts and shows understanding of the perspectives in both texts.

DOIT!

Write at least two detailed paragraphs comparing the methods the two cookery texts use to convey their ideas and perspectives. Use the student's notes from the table on page 69 to help you. Use the mark scheme and prompts in the question to guide your writing.

STRETCHIT!

Often, a writer's point of view is only fully appreciated across a whole text, rather than just in individual words, phrases and sentences: structure does influence readers. For example, the introduction in Text 2 (page 67) – Nigella Lawson's recipe – is consistent in style and tone: it is warm, almost conspiratorial throughout – a personal relationship is built between Lawson and her readers. Her language is consistently sensual: 'ooze', 'soggily', and 'fabulous'. Looking at language patterns across a whole text is one way to boost your answer into the top band.

These patterns create a consistent tone, which in turn conveys the writer's perspective.

Always ask yourself these questions when comparing ideas and perspectives:

- Is the information in the two texts placed in a particular order? For example:

  - Does the text give just one opinion?

  - Does it offer a balanced point of view?

  - Does it change at any point in the text?

- Are there any words or phrases that are repeated throughout the text? (Such as: family language, violent images, extended metaphors.)

- What is the tone of the text? (For example, is it sombre, upbeat, ironic or enthusiastic?)

- Are there any links or changes between the first and the last paragraphs of the text?

✓ CHECK**IT!**

1 How many texts will you need to write about in the ideas and perspectives comparison question?

2 Writers' methods include form, structure and language. Which of these should you concentrate on most?

3 How much should you write for your answer to the ideas and perspectives comparison question?

4 When you read a whole text, one way of analysing and tracking the development of its ideas and perspective is to label each paragraph with a word or short phrase, summing up what the paragraph is about.

Look at the full text of Chief Seattle's speech that you studied part of earlier. Use a word or short phrase to sum up the key purpose of each paragraph. The first one is done for you.

When you have identified the purposes of each paragraph, you will be in a better position to meet some of the top band criteria. In particular, you will be better placed to compare ideas and perspectives in a perceptive way.

> " The President in Washington sends word that he wishes to buy our land. But how can you buy or sell the sky? The land? The idea is strange to us. If we do not own the freshness of the air and the sparkle of the water, ◄ — No one owns the land. how can you sell them? Every part of this earth is sacred to my people. Every shining pine needle, every humming insect. All are holy in the memory and experience of my people.
>
> We know the sap which courses through the trees as we know the blood that courses through our veins. We are part of the earth and it is part of us. The perfumed flowers are our sisters. The bear, the deer, the great eagle, these are our brothers. The rocky crests, the juices in the meadow, the body heat of a pony, and man, all belong to the same family.

CHECKIT! ✓

The shining water that moves in the streams and rivers is not just water, but the blood of our ancestors. If we sell you our land, you must remember that it is sacred. Each ghostly reflection in the clear waters of the lakes tells of events and memories in the life of my people. The waters murmur in the voice of my father's father. The rivers are our brothers. They quench our thirst. They carry our canoes and feed our children. So you must give to the river the kindness you would give any brother.

If we sell you our land, remember that the air is precious to us, that the air shares its spirit with all the life it supports. The wind that gave our grandfather his first breath also receives his last sigh. The wind also gives our children the spirit of life. So if we sell you our land, you must keep it apart and sacred, as a place where man can go to taste the wind that is sweetened by the meadow flowers.

Will you teach your children what we have taught our children? That the earth is our Mother? What befalls the earth befalls all the sons of the earth.

This we know: The earth does not belong to man, man belongs to the earth. All things are connected like the blood that unites us all. Man did not weave the web of life; he is merely a strand of it. Whatever he does to the web, he does to himself.

One thing we know: Our God is your God. The earth is precious to him and to harm the earth is to heap contempt on its Creator. Your destiny is a mystery to us. What will happen when the buffalo are all slaughtered? The wild horses tamed? What will happen when the secret corners of the forest are heavy with the scent of many men and the view of the ripe hills is blotted by talking wires? Where will the thicket be? Gone! Where will the eagle be? Gone! And what is it to say goodbye to the swift pony and the hunt? The end of living and the beginning of survival.

When the last red man has vanished with his wilderness, and his memory is only the shadow of a cloud moving across the prairie, will these shores and forests still be here? Will there be any of the spirit of my people left? We love this earth as a newborn loves its mother's heartbeat. So if we sell you our land, love it as we have loved it. Care for it as we have cared for it. Hold in your mind the memory of the land as it is when you receive it. Preserve the land for all children and love it, as God loves us all.

As we are a part of the land, you too are part of the land. This earth is precious to us. It is also precious to you. One thing we know: There is only one God. No man, be he Red Man or White Man, can be apart. We are all brothers.

Chief Seattle

AO4: Evaluating texts critically

Assessment objective 4 assesses your understanding of how writers use language to engage the reader. This is the 'evaluation' question, and it will be focused on two broad areas:

- the quality of the writing
- your response to the writing.

These might look like very different things, but in practice they are closely linked: readers only respond positively and with interest to good writing. The quality of the writing is a major factor in how the reader responds.

Here are two examples of evaluation questions:

> What do you think and feel about Jennifer Thompson's views about healthy eating?
>
> **OR**
>
> Jennifer Thompson attempts to engage the reader through her comments on food and diets.
>
> Evaluate how successfully this is achieved.

The evaluation question wants you to consider how successful the writer has been in engaging your interest. Partly this is about giving a thoughtful personal response. Partly it is about choosing evidence from the text to support your explanations. You need to appreciate what the writer is trying to do, and how they are trying to do it. That is also what you need to do for the ideas and perspectives question.

The golden rules for the evaluation question are:

- Read and understand the question carefully.
- Think about what impact or influence the writer is trying to have on you, the reader.
- Think about what is good about the writing: focus on the effects of the writing on the reader.
- Don't get carried away with your own opinions/feelings about the text.
- Use quotations from the text to support your own ideas.
- Use any prompts below the question to help plan and structure your response.

NAIL IT!

- All the work you have already done on preparing for questions on ideas and perspectives will help you to answer evaluation questions.

- Evaluation questions also offer a lot of marks, so make sure you answer in enough detail.

☞ AQA does not include an evaluation question on the **non-fiction** paper. (Their evaluation question is the last one in Section A of the fiction paper.)

☞ OCR blends the **perspectives** and evaluation questions into one, so that you have to **evaluate** both texts as you compare them.

DOIT!

Re-read Nigella Lawson's recipe for warm spiced cauliflower and chickpea salad with pomegranate seeds on page 67.

Below is what one student wrote about her response to the text, with some notes by an exam marker alongside.

Notice how the student focuses on:

• the impact the text has on her and other readers
• what she likes about the writing.

WORKIT!

Personal impact on the reader.

Not fair/valid comment because some people — including Lawson — DO use 'supper'.

Use of supporting evidence, including quotations.

What the student likes and why.

When I read this recipe I can hear Nigella speaking as I have often seen her on TV and she always talks in this teasing, flirtatious way that many people think is odd for a cookery programme about food! Sometimes her vocabulary doesn't really work – 'suppers', for example. People don't use that word any more – they'd say dinner or tea. I love the tone of the writing though. I could read this sort of thing all day even if I wasn't going to actually cook anything. Nigella is always amusing. Treating the ingredients in an inappropriate sensual way is funny: 'the tomatoes almost ooze', and she keeps using the word 'toss' in a suggestive way. Lots of her language is teasing, almost as though the ingredients are ridiculous humans. When she says 'when the cauliflower has had its 15 minutes' you can immediately hear the implied words 'of fame' on the end – as though the cauliflower is showing off. I think that people who don't like cooking might be encouraged to try by this recipe because it is engaging and it sounds like you don't have to be too perfect about how you do it. On the other hand, the structure of the method is very formal and easy to follow, with its imperative verbs and numbered steps. This combination of eccentric, colourful language and a formal structure might well help non-cooks to start.

NAILIT!

You must use evidence from the text(s) – including quotations – to support your points.

Mark scheme for evaluating texts critically (AO4)

SNAPIT! Mark scheme for evaluating texts critically (AO4)

Mark scheme level	Band 2 (Roughly GCSE grades 2–3)	Band 3 (Roughly GCSE grades 4–6)	Band 4 (Roughly GCSE grades 7–9)
The student's answer...	• makes some comments that evaluate the text and begin to engage with its feelings/ideas • makes some relevant references to evidence in the text • comments on the writer's methods.	• critically evaluates the text and clearly engages with its feelings/ideas • makes well-chosen, effective references to evidence in the text, including quotations • explores and evaluates the effects of the writer's methods.	• persuasively evaluates the text and shows engagement and involvement with its feelings/ideas • gives well-selected examples and purposeful textual references to explain views convincingly • persuasively evaluates the effects of a range of the writer's choices • gives a perceptive overview of the text, its views and its impact.

CHECKIT!

1 What are the golden rules for evaluation questions?

2 Write some advice for the student who wrote the sample answer on page 74. Mention both strengths in the answer, and areas they could improve on. Take account of:

- the 'golden rules'
- the marker's notes
- your understanding of the mark scheme.

3 Read the student's answer on page 74 again. Decide which band you would place this answer in.

Non-fiction: Reading

1 How long should you spend on Section A, including reading and planning?

2 Will any of the texts on the paper have been written before 1900?

3 Which of the following is the main focus of the questions on this paper?

 a The information the writers give me.

 b The attitudes of the writers and how they try to influence me.

 c How much I agree with the writers.

4 In which of the statements below do we have to infer that the writer hates the music?

 a I hated that tune.

 b The music left me with a sense of loathing.

 c Whenever I heard that song I put my hands over my ears and screamed.

5 In all questions, are marks awarded:

 a for the number of the points you make, or

 b for the quality and relevance of your answer?

6 Write down seven useful words and phrases that help you to compare or contrast.

7 How many texts will you be asked about in the language and structure question?

8 Which of the following is the main focus of the language and structure question?

 a Information   c Language devices

 b Text structure   d The effects of language and structure choices.

9 In the following student's answer, find an example of evidence, and an example of subject terminology.

> To strengthen his argument by appealing to our emotions, Chief Seattle uses a sequence of personal pronouns: 'my', 'our', 'you'. Not only does this...

10 What does 'convey' mean?

11 Read the following text and choose which word best fits the writer's perspective on car drivers:

> Do they really need to keep jumping in their cars to satisfy every whim? Is burning up precious fossil fuel and polluting the planet a reasonable alternative to making the effort to walk round to the local shop?

 a love   c disapproval

 b dislike   d approval.

12 In the text used in Question 13 above, what persuasive technique is used twice? What effect does this have on the reader?

Non-fiction: Writing

Introduction and advice

The writing task appears on the paper as Section B. It comes straight after the reading questions in Section A and will be linked to an aspect of the texts in Section A; probably the topic. This will help you with content for your own writing in Section B.

The focus of the paper will be on **transactional writing**, such as persuasive and discursive writing. Essentially this is non-fiction with a real-world focus. It is writing 'with a job to do'. The job – the purpose – will be stated in the task on the paper.

In the writing section of the non-fiction exam, you will be tested against the following assessment objectives:

- Communicate clearly, effectively and imaginatively, selecting and adapting tone, style and register for different forms, purposes and audiences.
- Organise information and ideas, using structural and grammatical features to support coherence and cohesion of texts.

Candidates must use a range of vocabulary and sentence structures for clarity, purpose and effect, with accurate spelling and punctuation.

NAILIT!

Spend 45 minutes to an hour on planning, writing and checking your writing:

- Planning:
  5–10 minutes

- Writing:
  30–45 minutes

- Checking, correcting and improving:
  5 minutes

Remember! Checking your work to correct any errors will make sure you gain as many marks as possible.

Differences between the exam boards

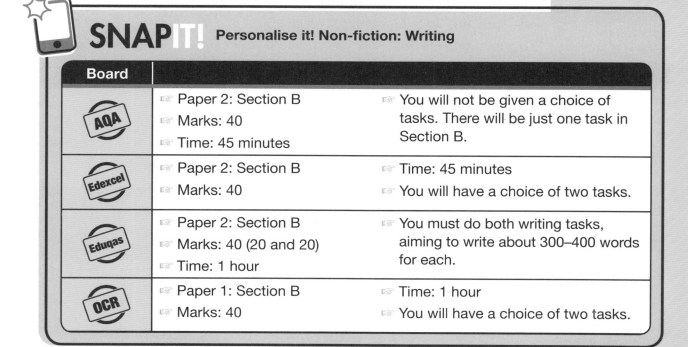

SNAPIT! **Personalise it! Non-fiction: Writing**

Board		
AQA	☞ Paper 2: Section B ☞ Marks: 40 ☞ Time: 45 minutes	☞ You will not be given a choice of tasks. There will be just one task in Section B.
Edexcel	☞ Paper 2: Section B ☞ Marks: 40	☞ Time: 45 minutes ☞ You will have a choice of two tasks.
Eduqas	☞ Paper 2: Section B ☞ Marks: 40 (20 and 20) ☞ Time: 1 hour	☞ You must do both writing tasks, aiming to write about 300–400 words for each.
OCR	☞ Paper 1: Section B ☞ Marks: 40	☞ Time: 1 hour ☞ You will have a choice of two tasks.

Here are the sorts of writing tasks you might be asked to do:

- Write a speech persuading readers that a wind farm should/not be built in your area.
- Write a report for your governors on how electricity could be saved in your school.
- Write a report advising old people on how to stay fit.
- Write a letter to the council outlining different opinions on a proposed new housing development.

The task will tell you the context for your writing. The context is the audience, purpose and form. The audience will always require you to write formally and for a purpose, such as:

- to explain
- to instruct or advise
- to argue
- to persuade.

The form could be:

- a letter
- an article (for example, for a newspaper or magazine)
- the text for a leaflet
- a speech
- an essay.

You need to plan your writing, and its style, so that it is just right for the given audience, purpose and form.

There are 40 marks for the writing task:

- 24 marks for communication and organisation (AO5)
- 16 marks for vocabulary, sentence structure, spelling and punctuation (VSSSP) (AO6).

Communication is about your ideas and how you express yourself so that you 'connect' with your reader (audience).

Organisation is about how you structure your content: paragraphs, sections, openings and closings, and so on.

VSSSP is about spelling, punctuation and grammar, and about using effective sentences and vocabulary. (See the vocabulary, sentence structure, spelling and punctuation (VSSSP) section starting on page 93.)

The mark scheme for non-fiction writing is the same as the mark scheme for fiction writing on page 35.

DOIT!

On a sticky note, write seven bullet points summing up the essential dos and don'ts for being successful in this task. Stick the note somewhere you will often see it.

CHECKIT! ✓

1 How many marks are available for the non-fiction writing section?

2 How many marks are available for VSSSP?

3 How many writing tasks will be on the paper for you to choose from?

4 What are the purposes that could be in the writing task?

5 Which of the following three forms will not be in the writing task?

- speech
- article
- story.

Language

The non-fiction writing section of the exam tests your understanding of assessment objective 5, or how effectively you can communicate your own personal view in a formal way. Therefore, you will need to organise your writing well and use formal language and tone.

Here are two versions of the same leaflet. One of them is written in an appropriate register; the other one is not.

WORKIT!

Student answer A

Welcome to this unique and treasured private garden, tucked serenely into a secret corner of our beautiful countryside.

Student answer B

Hey! Come on in! We're just loving our private garden that's quiet and all in this corner of our countryside.

1 The sentences below have been written for a head teacher (the 'audience').

My mates and me get loads of homework. That's not right cause it makes us stressed. We already have enough stuff to do in school :(:(We don't want no more homework being set by teachers.

Rewrite these sentences in Standard English – formal English.

2 Find some non-fiction texts and try rewriting parts of them so that they contain the same information but use inappropriate tone and language. This is a useful way of showing yourself how important it is to get the register right.

Preparation

Read the writing task very carefully. Spend a minute preparing the question and making sure you fully understand it.

Here is another example non-fiction writing question:

An environmental charity has launched an essay writing competition on the following issue:

'The earth does not belong to us: we belong to the earth.'

Write an article explaining your viewpoints about humans' relationship with the planet.

NAILIT!

Preparing the question must be quick, which is why it is worth practising.

That way you will get quicker at it.

The question starts with some background information to give you a context for your opinions. The actual thing you must do is printed below the information. Make sure that you identify the specific audience, purpose and form for the writing. In this task they are:

- audience (reader/s): judges of a writing competition
- purpose: to explain (your points of view) or to persuade
- form: an article.

There is another layer to preparing a question though: you also need to jot down some of your own thoughts, questions and useful vocabulary.

Here is how one student annotated the question:

> *Are the people who think we are ruining the earth experts?*
>
> *Adult judges?*
>
> *What does this mean? Do I agree? Is this about how people use the planet's resources?*

An environmental charity has launched an essay writing competition on the following issue:

'The earth does not belong to us: we belong to the earth.'

Write an article explaining your viewpoints about humans' relationship with the planet.

> *Outlining opinions with explanation, examples, arguments, beliefs and values.*

This student marked up the question as a form of one-minute preparation. You will notice that as part of their preparation, this student has written down words they think will be useful. Many of these are synonyms for key words in the question. Synonyms are words that mean roughly the same thing: for example, big/large; violence/force; woman/female.

Here is another non-fiction writing question:

> A school is reviewing its school uniform policy and has asked students for their views.
>
> Write a letter to the governors at your school, arguing for or against school uniform.

DO IT!

Write down some synonyms for these two words:

- relationship
- belong.

DO IT!

1 Copy out the question and prepare it as above.
2 Identify the audience, the purpose and the form in this writing task.

CHECK IT! ✓

1 What is Standard English?
2 How long should you spend preparing the question?
3 What is a synonym and why are synonyms important when preparing the question?

Planning

You should spend between five and ten minutes planning the content, structure and tone for your writing. It is necessary to spend this long as **good planning supports well-organised, clear and relevant ideas**.

Think back over all the advice you have received about planning during your GCSE course. Also look at any planning you have done. This process will help you work out the best ways to plan, and those areas where you have weaknesses and have not been effective enough in the past.

One good way to appreciate the importance of planning is to take a published text and then 'back plan' from it. To do this you should identify where the different sections of the text begin and then try to decide what the key purpose of that section is. When a text is in paragraphs, it is easy to spot the sections as they begin where paragraphs begin.

Here are two paragraphs from a non-fiction text:

> However delicious, burgers are certainly not without their downside. Most notable is their typical nutritional content. Quite frankly, the average burger's fat and calorie levels should make even the most dedicated junk-food lover have second thoughts about eating them. For example, one well-known brand's burger-with-cheese combo throbs with nearly 765 calories and 46 grams of fat, placing it well above the competition's burgers. Personally that makes me feel sick, and if an early heart attack is on your wish list, then I'd go ahead and order the double with cheese. This feast contains a staggering 1024 calories, 71 grams of fat, and 177 milligrams of cholesterol! Keep a paramedic handy for that one.
>
> So what's on offer if you're hankering after low-fat fast food? Well, not much. The only items reasonably low in calories and fat tend to be chicken sandwiches – as long as you do without the mayonnaise. Of course, you could order your beef burger without the cheese. This could cut the calories to 505 and the fat to 19 grams, which isn't too bad. However, I'd hesitate to recommend a burger without the cheese or mayonnaise. It really wouldn't taste of much.

We could sum up the topic of the first paragraph with the words 'nutritional content'. It's worth noting something else about the structure of the text these two paragraphs are from: the first paragraph above seems to begin with a link to the previous paragraph, and that paragraph was presumably about the taste of burgers.

NAILIT!

All writers produce much better work when they plan. This is because the content and its order is decided before writing begins, and that allows the writer to concentrate on expression as they write.

DO IT!

1 What is the topic of the second paragraph in the extract on page 81? Use no more than three words.
2 Gather together a variety of non-fiction texts (such as leaflets, articles, advice sheets) and back plan them. Spot and label the topic of each of their sections, and note any connections between the sections. Why have the sections been put together in the order that they are?
3 Below is one way to plan any non-fiction text in which you are going to state and develop a point of view. This example is one student's six-paragraph plan for a letter to the governors about school uniform. It is not complete. Copy it out and add detail to it.

WORK IT!

Introduction:

Explain which side I'm on. Show respect for the opposite view...

Dear Governors... I would like to put forward my views on... while I realise that...

Point 1:

Uniform is uncomfortable... It gets in the way of concentration...

Point 2:

Choice of clothes is an expression of identity... Creativity... Individuality

Point 3:

Point 4:

Acknowledge other side just to reject it. 'I know that some people say that...' However... Despite that... Use rhetorical question... If it's really true that... then why...?

Conclusion:

Thank you for reading... Giving me your time and attention... I do hope that...

Yours faithfully...

The opening

The first paragraph of your writing is crucial. You will need to reassure the exam marker that you can get your style, tone and vocabulary right for the task you have been given. In the opening, you must think carefully about your audience, purpose and form, and make sure your language is right for them.

DOIT!

Below are three different students' opening lines for the school uniform task on page 80. Read the three versions, and, as you read, think about how well the writing fits the advice you have already read. Try to put these three openings in order from best to worst. Write down your reasons for this order.

WORKIT!

Student answer A

Governors, you might like to wear fuddy old clothes but we do not. I've seen you wandering round the school like confused old crows, but there's no need to make us be the same as you. You're probably just jealous anyway. Cut us some slack! That's what I say, and now I'm gonna argue about it for you. By the time I've finished my argument you are going to think you've been stupid all these years you've made us wear the horrible stuff.

Student answer B

Dear governors,

I know that you have carefully debated the school uniform issue and have decided to keep it. I quite agree with you: I like wearing my own kit out of school but having to choose what to wear every day at school would be a total nightmare. I think that wearing school uniform means one less thing to worry about in the mornings, and that means there is more space in our minds for learning. Who in their right mind would want to do anything that crowds out learning? So, yes – let's keep school uniform: let's carry on concentrating on what really matters. Why would we want it any other way?

Student answer C

Dear Governors,

I realise that you believe that school uniform is important because it allows us all to focus on our work rather than on fashion and other matters that many adults would consider trivial. I understand where you are coming from: I know that you really do have our best interests at heart, and you sincerely want us to succeed and go on to lead happy and successful lives. However, I would like to put forward arguments for why all those great aims could be achieved even by students who attend lessons in their own clothes. In fact, I am going to suggest that this freedom of expression might even boost achievement.

Below is part of one student's school uniform letter. A few relevant descriptors from the mark scheme have been pointed out in the margin.

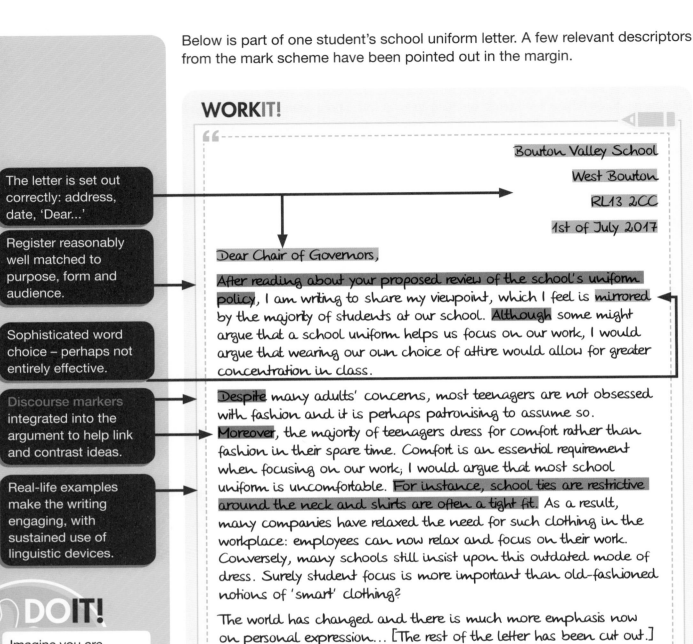

WORKIT!

> Bourton Valley School
> West Bourton
> RL13 2CC
> 1st of July 2017
>
> Dear Chair of Governors,
>
> After reading about your proposed review of the school's uniform policy, I am writing to share my viewpoint, which I feel is mirrored by the majority of students at our school. Although some might argue that a school uniform helps us focus on our work, I would argue that wearing our own choice of attire would allow for greater concentration in class.
>
> Despite many adults' concerns, most teenagers are not obsessed with fashion and it is perhaps patronising to assume so. Moreover, the majority of teenagers dress for comfort rather than fashion in their spare time. Comfort is an essential requirement when focusing on our work; I would argue that most school uniform is uncomfortable. For instance, school ties are restrictive around the neck and shirts are often a tight fit. As a result, many companies have relaxed the need for such clothing in the workplace: employees can now relax and focus on their work. Conversely, many schools still insist upon this outdated mode of dress. Surely student focus is more important than old-fashioned notions of 'smart' clothing?
>
> The world has changed and there is much more emphasis now on personal expression... [The rest of the letter has been cut out.]
>
> Yours faithfully,
>
> Ms Mary Meadows (Year 11)

Margin comments:

- The letter is set out correctly: address, date, 'Dear...'
- Register reasonably well matched to purpose, form and audience.
- Sophisticated word choice – perhaps not entirely effective.
- Discourse markers integrated into the argument to help link and contrast ideas.
- Real-life examples make the writing engaging, with sustained use of linguistic devices.
- Letter signed off correctly.

DOIT!

Imagine you are marking this letter. Add a few helpful comments for the student to help them improve the writing. Use the mark scheme on page 35 to guide your comments.

CHECKIT! ✓

1 How long should you spend making your plan?

2 What are the benefits of planning?

Context

You can simplify the mark scheme for AO5 into a few key elements that are easy to hold in your mind:

Communication

- clear and effective style
- using appropriate language choices
- effective vocabulary
- a range of linguistic devices used well.

Organisation:

- detailed and well-connected ideas
- well-organised paragraphs
- effective use of varied structural features.

The three elements of the context of the writing task are **audience, purpose and form**.

It's worth repeating that whatever combination of these appears in the exam question, the mark scheme is the same and your job will be to state, organise and develop an effective viewpoint.

Audience

The transactional writing task will suggest an audience for the writing. The audience will almost certainly change from year to year. However, the mark scheme will always require formal writing, and so the audience stated does not have an enormous significance for your own language choices. Here are three example tasks with the audience highlighted, and a brief explanation of why a formal style of writing would be needed.

1 Write the text of a speech for a debate at your school or college in which you persuade young people to become more involved in their local communities.

You might think that because the audience is young, you can use very informal language. That would be a mistake. The language should be formal because a school debate is formally organised. Your speech could include some words and phrases that might be expected to appeal strongly to that age group, but such words should be carefully chosen for effect and should be the exception, not the rule.

2 Write a letter to your local newspaper in which you argue for or against provision of a travellers' camp in your area.

Here, the audience is the readers of the local paper. They will tend to be adults, and almost all of them will be strangers to you. It would be rude and inappropriate to use informal language, and your arguments would sound less convincing.

> 3 Write an article for a national newspaper in which you explain your point of view about Britain's membership of the European Union.

Clearly, if you have been chosen to write an article for a national newspaper such as the *Daily Mail* or *The Times*, then you would be expected to use formal language. Again, it would be seen as inappropriate to use informal language.

Read the two different pieces of writing below. One is inappropriate and informal. The other is formal and much more interesting.

> **A**
>
> Get on down with the old folks in your area. You can help them with their rubbish computer skills, unwrap their manky sweets for them if they've got stiff fingers, and you could even chuck their rubbish out for them if they're too tired or lazy to do it for themselves.

> **B**
>
> There are many ways we could be helpful to old people living in our neighbourhood. Being helpful is not just about carrying out dull chores every week, such as making sure the rubbish is put outside for collection, and helping with a few routine jobs around the home. Being helpful can be about just reassuring them that they are not alone, and that they don't have to live out their lives in boredom and lonely isolation.

Purpose

The non-fiction writing question will target a purpose:

1. to explain
2. to instruct or advise
3. to discuss/argue
4. to persuade.

Whatever the purpose, you must give a clear point of view, with arguments and evidence, using language that is quite formal. However, it is worth considering some of the common features of each of these four purposes:

1 Writing to explain (your point of view)

- Start with a paragraph introducing your viewpoint.
- Give detailed reasons for your opinions.
- Give the reader information that supports your opinions (anecdotes, statistics, facts).
- Use a less passionate tone than if you were arguing or persuading.
- Sum up your key points at the end.

2 Writing to instruct or advise (helping your reader)

- Suggest things to the reader. (It would be a good idea to… You might want to…)
- Give some choices to the reader. (Alternatively, you could…)

NAILIT!

Write formally so that you sound trustworthy, but you still need to use a range of techniques to make your writing interesting.

- Share your opinions, but not too forcefully. (It's generally accepted that…)
- Use a tone that reassures the reader. (It's very common to feel…)
- Address the reader directly. (Use personal pronouns like 'you'.)
- Sum up your key points at the end. (Finally, the following points are important, remember to…)

3 Writing to discuss/argue (presenting a viewpoint with reasons)

- Present your opinions confidently.
- Keep your tone calm and polite – don't go on a rant.
- Use rhetorical devices to win your reader over (for example, rhetorical questions or repetition).
- Use connectives to link your ideas (however… similarly… although… as a result… in addition).
- Consider both sides of the argument (but stick to one side if the question tells you to do so).
- Use facts and statistics to support your points.
- Come to a conclusion after considering the facts (if you are considering both sides).

4 Writing to persuade (convincing your reader/changing your reader's mind)

If you are writing to persuade, you are aiming to convince the audience to agree with your viewpoint. Writing to argue and writing to persuade share many of the same features.

- Present your opinions strongly: aim to change your reader's opinion.
- Use rhetorical devices (like exaggeration, repetition, rhetorical questions).
- Criticise – and even mock – viewpoints that contradict your own.
- Use imperative verbs (do not believe; forget what others say…)
- Present opinions as facts (the strongest evidence to support this is…)
- Use emotive language (words chosen for their emotional impact on the reader).

DO IT!

Below are four sentences. Each sentence is from a text with a different purpose. Read each sentence carefully and decide which one of the four purposes it best matches.

a Smoking is a silent killer, rotting your internal organs and poisoning those around you.

b As students, there are lots of ways to save money. You could use the discounts offered by many clothing shops, cinemas or leisure centres.

c The first reason I do not like social media is because it can waste a great deal of time.

d Recently, scientific studies have made us think again about the wisdom of using diesel fuel.

DO IT!

Here is the first paragraph from a student's persuasive writing:

> If you think that wearing a uniform is a good idea, then you are crazy. School uniform is terrible. There are lots of reasons why it's terrible. For example, most people don't like it. I don't like it. If you think it's a good idea, then you're just wrong. I hate school uniform.

What makes this writing persuasive?

How could this persuasive writing be improved? (Look again at the mark scheme.)

DO IT!

Look back over your work from your English lessons. How many linguistic devices can you remember? List them in a table like the one opposite. Next to each device, write what it means and – if possible – give an example.

DO IT!

Think back over all the work you have done in English language, and then make a list of the key features of each form. Don't look at the suggestions on the next few pages until you have made your own list. The table below contains a few suggestions to start you off.

Linguistic devices

To make your writing interesting and engaging you must use a range of appropriate linguistic devices. There are an infinite number of linguistic devices, but some are very popular with non-fiction writers.

Device	Explanation	Example
Rhetorical question	A question is asked but no reply is needed.	'Do you think I'm stupid?'
Alliteration	Words near each other, deliberately starting with the same sound so that they stand out.	The most important question is why can't we all be kind and considerate enough not to kill each other?

Form

You will be told clearly what form to write. The form could be:

- a formal letter
- an article (for a newspaper, magazine or website)
- the text for a leaflet
- a report
- a speech
- an essay.

The exam marker should be able to recognise the form you are using, so it is important that you use some of the key features of the form you are given.

Form	Formal letter	Article	Leaflet	Speech	Essay
Typical features	Your address at the top	Engaging title	Subheadings	Direct address to listeners	Introduction
	Dear…	An opening paragraph to introduce the topic	Sections	Summing up	Different paragraphs for subtopics

Here are some of the features that the exam markers will want to see for different forms:

SNAPIT!

Form	Features
Formal letter	<ul><li>'Dear…'</li><li>Paragraphs in an effective order</li><li>Addresses (e.g. yours and theirs)</li><li>Date</li><li>Yours sincerely or faithfully, as appropriate</li></ul>
Article	<ul><li>An engaging title (e.g. to catch the reader's attention and introduce your point)</li><li>A strapline – a very short, snappy summary of the article under the title</li><li>An opening paragraph that provides an overview of the subject</li><li>Subheadings</li><li>An introductory paragraph</li><li>Paragraphs in an effective order</li></ul>
Text for a leaflet	<ul><li>A title that is clear, engaging and appropriate</li><li>Subheadings</li><li>Paragraphs or sections</li><li>Paragraphs in an effective order</li><li>Bullet points</li></ul>
Speech	<ul><li>A clear address to the audience (e.g. Welcome, ladies and gentlemen, it is an honour to stand in front of you all today…)</li><li>A clear signing off (e.g. Thank you for sitting through these important ideas and I hope they will fill your thoughts on your way home…)</li><li>Rhetorical devices to engage the listener throughout</li><li>Sections/paragraphs in an effective order</li><li>A final address to the audience/summing up</li></ul>
Report	<ul><li>An introduction (your introduction would normally focus on the topic you have researched)</li><li>Linked paragraphs in an effective order</li><li>A conclusion (e.g. Finally… In conclusion… To conclude… In summary…)</li></ul>

DO IT!

1 Find some examples of each of the five forms on page 89. See how many of the features listed you can find in the examples.
2 Note down any other common features you find for each form. Plan to use some of these in your own writing in the exam.
3 Create a revision poster for each form of writing. List the main features and include images and diagrams to remind you of the key ideas.

In the exam, whatever the form you are given in the non-fiction writing task, don't waste any time drawing detailed images or diagrams, or making your title attractive with colours and special writing. You won't be given any marks for these fancy features.

CHECK IT! ✓

1 True or False?

a You should spend time making the text look nice with special writing, fonts and colours.

b Articles should contain a strapline.

c You should start your speech with speech marks.

d You can choose which form to use in the exam.

e An essay should start with an introduction.

f If you start a letter with 'Dear Madam' you should finish with 'Yours sincerely'.

2 Below are three tasks with different combinations of purpose, audience and form. For each of the three tasks, write the first 30–70 words, using language appropriate to the context.

a A letter to your head teacher/principal explaining why you need a week off school/college.

b A leaflet advising old people on how to stay fit and active.

c An article in a free magazine persuading visitors of the advantages of your local area.

1 What is transactional writing?

2 How long must you leave for the writing task?

3 How long should you leave for checking your writing at the end?

4 The writing task will include a context for your writing. What three things comprise the context?

5 Whatever the context of the writing task, the main focus is always the same. What is that focus?

6 List four possible purposes that the writing task covers.

7 List the five possible forms that the writing task could take.

8 Identify the purpose and form in this exam question:

> Write an advice leaflet for the teachers of foreign students who will be visiting your local town to improve their English.

9 Communication is one focus of the mark scheme. What are the other two focuses?

10 Explain which of the following two text extracts is more formal:

> **A**
>
> This is a very safe town, and there are very few precautions you will need to take. As long as your students follow a few simple rules and look after their belongings, then they will come to no harm.

> **B**
>
> This town is as safe as anything. The kids just need to behave themselves – no messing about – and they'll be ok.

11 What should you do when you prepare the question?

12 Write at least one synonym for each of the following words:
   - audience
   - purpose
   - form.

13 Why might you acknowledge an opposing view in your writing?

14 Write down at least two benefits of planning.

15 Briefly explain what is good about this opening and how it might be improved:

> I hope your students will feel safe and happy in my town. I bet you will. There's really nothing much for you to worry about. In fact, it's a great place.

16 What should you bear in mind in the first paragraph of your writing?

17 What are the key elements of the mark scheme?

18 Which one of the four purposes is this writing for?

> Many parents worry about how closely they should supervise their children's leisure activities. On one hand, you want to be able to trust your children and give them the freedom to develop. On the other hand, you are responsible for their safety.

19 Which of the following questions is likely to be rhetorical? Explain why.

a Do you know when the bus is coming?

b Don't you just hate it when buses don't turn up?

c Which stop are you getting off at?

d Is this the right bus?

e Why does it always rain when I'm waiting for the bus?

20

> 'Prison is both cruel and pointless, and costs the rest of us a great deal of money. There are much better ways of dealing with people who are convicted of crimes.'
>
> Write the text of a leaflet in which you persuade readers of your views on how we should deal with people found guilty of less serious crimes.

Writing: Vocabulary, sentence structure, spelling and punctuation (VSSSP)

Introduction and advice

VSSSP covers a number of aspects including spelling, punctuation and grammar. VSSSP is extremely important as it accounts for a lot of marks. In the writing sections of both exam papers, VSSSP (assessment objective 6) accounts for 40 per cent of the marks. Even in the English Literature exams some marks are given (or lost) for VSSSP.

The six key aspects of VSSSP are:

1 Sentence demarcation

2 Punctuation

3 Sentences

4 Standard English

5 Spelling

6 Vocabulary

To get the most marks possible, you need to use all six aspects accurately, appropriately and effectively.

Sentence demarcation

Put simply, sentence demarcation is about using capital letters and full stops to mark the beginnings and ends of sentences. Sentences can also end with exclamation marks and question marks, where appropriate. It is very important that you use some of the time in the examination to re-check you have accurately used capital letters and punctuation at the ends of sentences.

Below is some writing by a student. Five capital letters, three full stops, one question mark and one exclamation mark have been removed.

WORKIT!

we cannot go on spoiling the planet we live on in just a few decades we have dug up and burnt the fossil fuels that nature took millions of years to create how much longer will we be able to carry on doing this we must stop it now our children and grandchildren will not thank us for using up all the planet's resources before they are even born

DO IT!

Copy out the writing and put in the sentence demarcations as you go.

DO IT!

Copy out each text, writing in the capital letters and ending the sentences with either a full stop, an exclamation mark or a question mark, as appropriate.

Below are extracts from two different sorts of texts: a novel and an advertisement. In both cases, the capital letters and punctuation have been left out so that the beginning and end of the sentences are not shown.

> ### Novel extract
>
> javad stretched and yawned he could hardly keep his eyes open how would he ever stay awake until morning and the safety of daylight he had promised to keep watch but now his will was weakening he edged a few inches away from the fire perhaps coldness would fight tiredness he knew that he and James would both rather be cold than dead

> ### Advertisement extract
>
> come alive with zingo fizz zingo fizz is the tingling new soft drink that will make you glad to be young if you're not young then zingo will make you think you are what could be wrong with that drink zingo it's good to be young even if you're not

DO IT!

Find a variety of texts: newspaper articles, leaflets, novels, and so on, and look carefully at how the beginnings and endings of sentences are marked. Note how sentences can be long, medium or even very short. Which sorts of text are most likely to use question marks or exclamation marks?

Punctuation

The exam marker is looking for a range of accurately used punctuation. This is because punctuation is one important way that a writer guides and controls the reader's reaction. Good writers use punctuation to make the reader pause, and to emphasise certain details for meaning and effect.

Punctuation is not just a matter of accuracy: it is also a matter of style and effect. In the exercise above, you probably found that punctuation is used in different ways for different purposes at different times. Writers use punctuation to help the reader and also to control how the reader reads. For example, sometimes writers use punctuation to make the reader pause so that they will notice an important detail.

Here is an extract from the novel *Never Let Me Go* by Kazuo Ishiguro:

> Usually we just spread ourselves around the chairs and benches – there'd be five of us, six if Jenny B. came along – and had a good gossip. There was a kind of conversation that could only happen when you were hiding away in the pavilion; we might discuss something that was worrying us, or we might end up screaming with laughter, or in a furious row. Mostly, it was a way to unwind for a while with your closest friends.

In this one short paragraph the novelist, Ishiguro, has used:

- two dashes
- four full stops
- four commas
- one semicolon.

Here is an example of a student analysing one of Ishiguro's uses of punctuation:

WORKIT!

The writer, Ishiguro, uses a dash after 'benches'. This dash makes a pause as though the narrator is having a sudden extra thought, but pausing only very briefly. A full stop might have suggested that the narrator was calmer, less rushed.

Notice that Ishiguro writes some quite long stretches of words without any punctuation at all. The longest of these unpunctuated stretches is 18 words.

DOIT!

1 Read the extract from *Never Let Me Go* on page 94. Try to explain the purpose of each piece of punctuation.
2 Could Ishiguro have used any punctuation in those 18 words? If so, where, and why? Which works better: with punctuation or without? Why?
3 Now find short extracts (of about 50 words) from good examples of at least three of these different sorts of text:
   • fiction
   • a letter
   • an article from a newspaper, magazine or website
   • a leaflet
   • a speech
   • an essay.
   Underline all the punctuation marks in each short extract and explain the purpose of each one.
   Doing this research task will make you more aware of how punctuation is actually used. It will help you to understand that punctuation is not just used to obey rules: often it is used for deliberate effect.

Comma (,)

The comma is one of the most important pieces of punctuation. There are rules for where commas should be used. However, commas are actually used for three main purposes:

• To separate words in a list.

• To make the reader pause so that a detail can be emphasised.

• To make meaning clearer.

A comma must never be used instead of a full stop to end a statement; a complete statement is a sentence. It must end with a full stop.

• He walked over to his car, he got in. Wrong!

• He walked over to his car. He got in. Right!

• She was late, however no one minded. Wrong!

• She was late. However, no one minded. Right!

• He left the room, she followed. Wrong!

• He left the room. She followed. Right!

Look again at the different sorts of text you have gathered earlier in this section. Find a few commas in each text. Decide what each comma has been used for. You might find that it has more purposes than the three already listed in this section.

DOIT!

Each sentence below uses a comma for one of the three purposes. Decide which purpose is shown by the comma(s) in each sentence.

1 Having first tried to hide and control his panic, Imran finally decided to run.
2 It was going to be a long, boring, tiring and unpleasant day.
3 On Thursday it was sunny and bright, and rainy and cold was how Friday started out.

DO IT!

Which two of the following are punctuated correctly?

a It was a hot day, no one could be bothered to work.

b The dog ran, barked, jumped and then went still and quiet.

c I love chocolate. I'm going to buy some.

d We left the house, we never went back.

DO IT!

Go back over the different sorts of text you have gathered. Find examples of commas used to start sentences with non-essential detail.

Using a comma with fronted subordinate clauses and phrases

Sometimes we want to start a sentence with a non-essential detail, rather than with the main information. Often we do this for dramatic effect – to make the reader wait.

Here are some examples:

> Having arrived in plenty of time, I was annoyed that the party had already started.
>
> Outside the house, under the bright stars, Tom and Sarah were falling in love.
>
> Although she was older than her sister, she never seemed to get the best presents or the best room.

Exclamation mark (!)

Exclamation marks add emphasis to a statement – for example, shock or surprise. Do not overuse the exclamation mark in your writing. **Never** use double exclamation marks!

Semicolon (;)

You should not overuse the semicolon, but it can be very useful when used occasionally.

A semicolon can be used for two main purposes:

1 To separate multi-word items in a list. For example:

> I bought six juicy, ripe peaches; some expensive, but very mature cheddar cheese; a kilo of sausages; and some milk.
>
> There are many ways to use stationery to make your revision more exciting: you could use a mixture of highlighter pens; a range of different sized sticky notes; different coloured plain and lined paper; and a range of different cards to make flash cards.

2 To join two sentences that belong to each other in some way, perhaps by explaining each other. For example:

> He was not wearing his best jacket; he always looked scruffy.
>
> Revising is most effective when done in short bursts; research has shown that concentration wanders if you revise for long periods without a break.

In the second example above, the semicolon has been used instead of the word 'because'; the statement on one side of the semicolon explains the statement on the other side.

However, you will probably find that different texts and authors use semicolons for a variety of purposes – not just the two main purposes explained here.

Colon (:)

A colon is used for two main purposes:

1. To introduce some information – usually some sort of list.

2. To mean 'that is to say' or 'in other words'.

Apostrophe (')

Apostrophes are mainly used in two ways:

1. To show omission.

2. To show possession.

Omission means to leave something out: the apostrophe is used to replace letters in a word. For example:

- *Would not* becomes *wouldn't*.

- *I do not* becomes *I don't*.

- *You are* becomes *you're*.

Possession means showing that one thing belongs to another. For example:

> Sarah's highlighter pen was missing.

The apostrophe is always placed straight after the 'owner' (possessor). That means that if the owner is a plural ending in 's', then the apostrophe should appear after the 's'. For example:

> The students' highlighter pens were missing.

In this example, the apostrophe tells us that the missing pens were owned by more than one student. If the apostrophe came before the 's' then we would know that all the pens were owned by just one unfortunate student.

NAIL IT!

It's and *its* are special cases. We use the apostrophe if the word means '*it is*', but we do not use the apostrophe if the word means '*of it*':

- It's a heavy kettle. (Omission: '*it's*' means '*it is*'.)
- He picked up the kettle by its handle. (Possession: the handle belongs to the kettle.)

DO IT!

Look through the texts you gathered for the sentence demarcation section. Find every semicolon. Try to decide why each one has been used. You will probably find that different writers use semicolons for slightly different purposes. You might find some texts where they are never used.

DO IT!

Rewrite the following sentences, adding, moving or removing the apostrophes as necessary.

a We cant go to Nelums' party because we promised wed visit our nan's house.
b Its important to eat lots of vegetable's.
c The students ideas for raising money were very imaginative.
d Chanelles' idea for raising money was the most popular.

Reviewing how you use (or don't use) punctuation is important: it allows you to spot which punctuation problems you should work on first so that you can control your writing better and gain more marks.

Look at examples of your own writing.

- What sorts of punctuation do you most often leave out or use incorrectly?
- Do you currently use the full range of punctuation marks?
- Which punctuation marks do you avoid?
- Which do you overuse?

CHECK IT! ✓

1 Punctuation should be used for accuracy. Name two other reasons for using punctuation.

2 What are the three purposes of a comma?

3 In which of the two sentences below should a comma have been used? Where should it have been used? Why?

   a Leaping in the air Sadia neatly caught the ball.

   b Sadia neatly caught the ball by leaping in the air.

4 One of the sentences below needs a colon. The other needs a semicolon. Write out the two sentences, putting in the correct punctuation. Explain why you have used the punctuation you have added into each sentence.

   a He got up late he missed the bus.

   b There was a reason he missed the bus he got up late.

5 In the following sentence two parents jointly own a car. Write out the sentence and put the apostrophe in the right place. Explain why you have placed the apostrophe where you have.

   "
   I was shocked when I saw his parents car.
   "

6 Copy out the text below and put the following pieces of punctuation in the right places.

   - four full stops
   - two commas
   - one semicolon
   - one colon.

   "
   Breathing heavily I came to a stop outside my destination the station I gasped for air my lungs were bursting although I had hardly got my breath back I forced my legs to take me onto the platform the train was coming in
   "

Sentences

You need to craft your sentences so that your language has an impact on the reader. The exam marker will be looking for a **variety** of sentence forms used for effect. If you only use simple sentences, or compound sentences connected with the word 'and', you will get very low marks for VSSSP.

Decide which of the following has a stronger impact on the reader:

> **A**
>
> Without a doubt, exercise is important. Eating healthily is important. Most crucially of all, we need to get enough sleep.

> **B**
>
> Exercise is really important and healthy eating is important and getting enough sleep is crucial.

Sentence variety is about using different types of sentence and the order of their parts to emphasise your main ideas and keep your writing interesting. In the examples above, the same information has been given in different ways. The first version is more engaging in terms of the types of sentence used and how they are organised.

Look at it again:

> Without a doubt, exercise is important.

This first sentence doesn't start with the main point, but with a dramatic emphasis, telling you that you can't disagree, even though you don't yet know what you **could** disagree with!

> Eating healthily is important.

This is a very short, assertive sentence.

> Most crucially of all, we need to get enough sleep.

Again, this final sentence does not start with the main point. 'Most crucially of all' creates a sort of dramatic pause that strengthens the main point when it arrives.

DOIT!

Here is something that a student wrote in an exam. Rewrite it so that its sentence variety is much more effective:

He ran quickly. He got to the safety of the big rock. He looked back at the people and he couldn't see them and he felt relieved and he drank some water.

STRETCHIT!

Varying sentences is a key marker of a good writer. Variety not only keeps your ideas interesting: variety also gives you the opportunity to influence your reader and give your ideas persuasive power.

Look at the two extracts from exam answers below. They are similar in content, but the style of version B is much more varied and is likely to have a much more powerful effect on the reader.

WORKIT!

Student answer A

Seventeen year olds are too young to be driving. Many seventeen year olds can hardly walk in a straight line. It's not a good idea to let them drive cars. They can be really dangerous.

Student answer B

Barely able to walk in a straight line half the time, teenagers would be lethal behind the wheel of a car, and – however grown up they consider themselves to be – seventeen year olds are still only teenagers. Let them wait a year before they get the licence to kill.

Discourse markers

Discourse markers are words and phrases used to connect and sequence ideas and information. They help you to link paragraphs, sentences and even different parts of sentences. They are, therefore, essential to achieving sentence variety. Here is a table of one type of discourse marker – connectives – sorted into categories:

NAILIT!

Discourse markers in the table below starting with a capital letter are normally only used at the start of a sentence:

- I wanted to go. *However*, I didn't feel well enough.

- I wasn't feeling well. *Therefore* I didn't go.

SNAPIT!

Cause and effect	Contrasting	Comparing	Time and sequence
because Therefore consequently so	In contrast whereas On the other hand Conversely However	Equally In comparison Likewise Similarly In the same way	while when since Next then Firstly
Adding	**Emphasising**	**Giving an example**	**Exceptions and conditions**
In addition Moreover Furthermore as well as What is more	Above all In particular especially	For example For instance as revealed by such as	although even though despite in spite of unless if

Standard English

In your English exams, you must write in Standard English. English is spoken in many versions (or 'dialects'). Because of this variety, there needs to be a standard version that everyone can understand. This is Standard English – a formal version of English that is used in business and all official communication. It is a polite form of language that should always be used between people who are not personal friends. Of course, it is not the form of English that is used between people who know each other well. Effective writers sometimes slip out of Standard English for effect. For example:

> Most people firmly believe that school uniform is crucial for the success of a school. It ain't necessarily so.

Here the writer has used the informal 'ain't' as a dramatic contrast with the previous very formal sentence.

Here, are some marking descriptors for sentences and Standard English:

Aspect	Band 2 descriptors (Roughly GCSE grades 2–3)	Band 3 descriptors (Roughly GCSE grades 4–6)	Band 4 descriptors (Roughly GCSE grades 7–9)
Sentences	The student's answer… • tries out different sentence forms	The student's answer… • varies sentences for effect	The student's answer… • uses a full range of appropriate sentence structures for effect
Standard English	• sometimes uses Standard English with some control of agreement.	• mostly uses Standard English appropriately and with controlled grammatical structures.	• always uses Standard English appropriately and with secure control of complex grammatical structures.

Here is part of a student's letter to the governors to ask for the sports centre to be rebuilt. Some comments by an exam marker are also shown.

NAIL IT!

Avoid using informal English. It really might not work. If in doubt, leave it out.

DO IT!

Which four of the following sentences use informal English?

a We were unable to go.
b Me and John went to the beach.
c He doesn't want to go shopping.
d She don't like curry.
e He was sat on the wall.
f We done it so badly.
g They did it well.

WORK IT!

The sports centre will be a ~~fab and~~ educational place for all ages and it will also provide a place where the community ~~can get down and get fit~~, whilst having fun. The sports centre will have loads of activities that children and adults can get involved with – swimming, five-a-side football, squash, basketball, yoga and zumba and many stuff. These activities will become available as soon as the sports centre will be opened.

> Odd mix of informal and formal vocabulary.

> Sentences are fluent but the first two start in the same way.

> More correct to say 'is opened'.

NAIL IT!

Notice how the main changes to the student's writing are to do with:

- appropriate vocabulary
- sentence structure (how they are arranged)
- verb forms (for example, 'would' rather than 'will').

Leave some time at the end of your writing tasks in the exam so you can check through your work to correct any mistakes.

This student can use formal vocabulary and can sustain long sentences, but is not consistent in how they use and control these elements. There is some variety of sentence structure, and some control of register (formal English).

This writing would belong in the bottom of Band 3. The exam marker suggested this slight improvement in the writing to raise it to the top of Band 3:

WORKIT!

An enjoyable and educational place for all ages, a new sports centre would also provide a place where the community can get down and get fit, whilst having fun. The sports centre would have a wide variety of activities that children and adults could get involved with, such as swimming, 5-a-side football, squash, basketball, yoga and zumba. These activities would become available as soon as the sports centre is opened.

CHECKIT!

1 Name two good reasons for varying your sentences.

2 Copy out the words below, completing them with two different discourse markers that make sense.

> " I was hungry I put two samosas in the oven. "

3 Here are three pieces of students' writing. As you read through them, compare them with the descriptors for sentences and for Standard English on page 101. Decide which band each piece belongs in. They all belong to different bands: 2, 3 or 4. Which is which?

CHECKIT!

Student answer A

Advertising can be a right pain and get in the way of everything but overall it's a great thing. If there wasn't any adverts then companies can't make us aware of their great products and they wouldn't be able to grow into successful companies.

Student answer B

I realise that money is in short supply and there are so many worthy causes to be considered. However, overall our school is already very successful and up to date, and it is full of facilities that we can feel very proud of: a state-of-the-art recording studio; a bright and comfortable dining area; an all-weather playing surface – facilities that might even be considered to be luxuries. We need a new sports centre as well.

Student answer C

I know teenagers that are under pressure to start a relationship just to prove that they are mature. I know one who really don't know what she's doing. She just keeps getting hurt. I know many adults who wasn't very sensible when they was young either, although my aunt and uncle got married before they was twenty and they are glad they done it.

DO IT!

Make a list of your five most frequent incorrect spellings.

NAIL IT!

- Learn key spellings as you revise.

- Highlight the tricky section of words you misspell.

- Don't forget to include spellings from your other GCSE subjects.

NAIL IT!

Even during your revision weeks, make some time to read quality fiction and non-fiction. Look up and learn words you don't know. Write down these words and their meanings on sticky notes and post them in places where you will see them regularly.

Spelling

Most people are better spellers than they think. Never be ashamed of your spelling. It's worth remembering that:

- English is a difficult language to spell

- many great writers are not great spellers

- spelling actually accounts for very few marks.

It is possible to get a mark for using a very good word even if you don't spell it correctly. However, students who are not confident about their spelling risk losing marks in other, related ways: they try to hide their spelling by using unclear handwriting or by using words that are too simple to be effective. Don't do that. Use the best word possible; write it clearly and spell it as well as you can.

Common mistake patterns

- Illogical spellings (such as, 'rember' instead of the correct 'remember').

- Homophone (same sound) mistakes (such as, 'their'/'there'/'they're' and 'new'/'knew').

- Combining words (such as, 'alot' instead of 'a lot').

- Contraction spelling mistakes (forgetting the apostrophe in 'don't' or 'I'll').

- Words that are missing a double letter (such as, 'finaly' instead of 'finally').

- Words given double letters by mistake (such as, 'untill' instead of 'until').

- A letter missed out by mistake (such as, 'belive' instead of 'believe').

- Letters reversed by mistake (such as, 'minuet' instead of 'minute').

- Using American spelling (such as, 'socialize' instead of 'socialise').

- Missing out silent letters (in words such as, 'parliament', 'government', 'Wednesday', 'science' and 'chocolate').

Spelling strategies

Here are some tricks to help you remember common spellings.

Necessary: a shirt has one **c**ollar and two **s**leeves (one c, two s).

Because: **b**ig **e**lephants **c**an **a**lways **u**nderstand **s**mall **e**lephants.

Vocabulary

The exam marker is looking for a range of vocabulary in your writing. The top marks in the exam will be given for 'wide and ambitious' vocabulary. However, it's important not to use complicated words if you're not sure of their meaning – being clear is more important.

- Avoid vague words (like 'big', 'ok', 'good' and 'nice').

- If it suits the form and purpose, use specialist words (like 'simile', 'environment' and 'identity').

- Try to choose words carefully to have an appropriate impact on the reader.

Mark scheme for VSSSP (AO6)

The mark scheme for VSSSP is the same for the writing tasks in both English Language papers. (There are no VSSSP marks to be won or lost when you are answering the reading questions.)

SNAPIT!

Aspect	Band 2 descriptors (Roughly GCSE grades 2–3)	Band 3 descriptors (Roughly GCSE grades 4–6)	Band 4 descriptors (Roughly GCSE grades 7–9)
Sentence demarcation	The student's answer… • marks the beginnings and ends of most sentences	The student's answer… • marks the beginnings and ends of almost all sentences	The student's answer… • correctly marks the beginnings and ends of sentences
Punctuation	• often uses basic punctuation well	• uses a range of punctuation usually correctly	• uses a wide range of punctuation almost always correctly
Sentences	• tries out different sentence structures and types	• varies sentences for effect	• uses a wide range of sentence structures confidently and effectively
Standard English	• sometimes uses Standard English, perhaps with some mistakes over agreement or tense endings	• mainly uses Standard English with good control and flexibility	• uses appropriate Standard English with control and flexibility throughout
Spelling	• sometimes spells more complex words correctly (such as 'height', 'definite')	• makes few spelling mistakes – even complex and irregular words (such as 'accommodation', 'rhythmic', 'parallel')	• spells almost all words correctly, including adventurous vocabulary (such as 'combustible', 'opprobrium', 'machination')
Vocabulary	• varies vocabulary.	• chooses some precise and sophisticated vocabulary.	• uses a wide and adventurous vocabulary.

✓ CHECKIT!

1 What are homophones?

2 Here are three spellings. Which one is correct?

  a disappear   **b** dissapear   **c** dissappear.

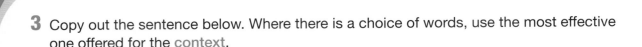

CHECK IT! ✓

3 Copy out the sentence below. Where there is a choice of words, use the most effective one offered for the **context**.

> She lay beneath the tree in <u>discomfort/pain/agony</u>, blood <u>dripping/oozing/coming</u> from the deep <u>wound/cut/gash</u> and soaking into the earth around her.

4 To get to know the mark scheme better, read the first part of a student's letter to the school governors about school uniform below. Here are some marker comments based on the mark scheme for VSSSP:

- Correct layout for formal letter.
- The opening uses Standard English.
- Ambitious vocabulary is correctly spelled.
- Sentence structure is used for effect.
- A wide range of punctuation is used (semicolons and colons).

a In the letter, find examples of each of the five marker comments.

b Find examples in the letter of other descriptors from the mark scheme for VSSSP.

> Welton Valley School
>
> West Bradley
>
> WS99 1BA
>
> 1st July 2019
>
> Dear Chair of Governors,
>
> After reading about your proposed review of the school's uniform policy, I am writing to share my viewpoint, which I feel is mirrored by the majority of students at our school. Although some might argue that a school uniform helps us focus on our work, I would argue that wearing our own choice of attire would allow for greater concentration in class.
>
> Despite many adults' concerns, most teenagers are not obsessed with fashion and it is perhaps patronising to assume so. Moreover, the majority of teenagers dress for comfort rather than fashion in their spare time. Comfort is an essential requirement when focusing on our work; I would argue that most school uniform is uncomfortable. For instance, school ties are restrictive around the neck and shirts are often a tight fit. As a result, many companies have relaxed the need for such clothing in the workplace: employees can now relax and focus on their work. Conversely, many schools still insist upon this outdated mode of dress. Surely student focus is more important than old-fashioned notions of 'smart' clothing?

5 Improve the letter by rewriting part of it and/or continuing it.

1 What percentage of the marks in the writing exams are accounted for by VSSSP?

2 Is VSSSP only about accuracy?

3 What are the six aspects of VSSSP?

4 What are the three pieces of punctuation that can end a sentence?

5 Name seven different punctuation marks.

6 Why is punctuation important?

7 Which of the following sentences uses a comma incorrectly?

   a He wrote his story, but his teacher didn't like it.

   b The sports centre is fun, it also helps us get fit.

   c Although he was ill, he didn't go to bed.

   d He found a beautiful, quiet, sandy, beach.

8 In which sentence below is the semicolon not used correctly?

   a He woke up while it was still dark; he went downstairs.

   b It was raining; he put on his coat.

   c She realised all these things: she was excited, happy and impatient; her mother was angry, and her father wasn't going to help.

9 What are the two reasons for using a colon?

10 In which sentences below is the apostrophe not used correctly?

   a Sadiq's uncle bought some potatoe's.

   b Its hot today.

   c The childrens teacher couldn't be found anywhere.

   d I picked up the kettle by it's handle.

   e The river's flow was'nt fast enough.

11 What is meant by 'sentence variety'?

12 Discourse markers are words and phrases that make connections in texts. There are at least eight discourse markers in the text below. Find all of them.

> This tiredness stayed with Errol all week. He didn't seem to be able to get out of bed. Even when Hayley knocked on the door and called through the letter box, he just couldn't stir himself. Nights and days slowly passed through his stuffy room like silent visitors. They didn't trouble him though. His eyes were closed and he was elsewhere in his head. Because of his fever, he often didn't really know where he was.

13 Which one of the following sentences is not written in Standard English?

   a She waved to John and me.

   b Zanira and I went to the cinema.

   c We wasn't speaking to each other.

   d I did it well.

14 Which four of the following words are not spelled correctly?

definitely   independant   business   trouble   hopefull

neccessary   because   dissappear   disappoint   accommodation

ENGLISH LITERATURE

Introduction and advice

This section will help you prepare for your English Literature GCSE exams. This is how the English Literature papers will be organised in the exams.

SNAPIT!

Exam board	Exam	Section A	Section B	Section C
AQA	Paper 1: Shakespeare and the 19th-century novel • 1 hour 45 minutes • 64 marks • 40% of GCSE	**Shakespeare** • Answer one question • 1 hour • 34 marks	**19th-century novel** • Answer one question • Your answer will be in the form of an essay • 45 minutes • 30 marks	**No section C**
	Paper 2: Modern texts and poetry • 2 hours 15 minutes • 96 marks • 60% of GCSE	**Modern prose or drama** • Answer one question • 45 minutes • 34 marks	**Poetry** • Answer one question • 45 minutes • 30 marks	**Unseen poetry** • Answer both questions • 45 minutes • 32 marks
Edexcel	Paper 1: Shakespeare and Post-1914 Literature • 1 hour 45 minutes • 80 marks • 50% of GCSE	**Shakespeare** • Answer a two-part question • Spend equal time on parts (a) and (b) • 55 minutes • 40 marks	**Post-1914 Literature** • Answer one question • 50 minutes • 40 marks	**No section C**
	Paper 2: 19th-century Novel and Poetry since 1789 • 2 hours 15 minutes • 80 marks • 50% of GCSE	**19th-century novel** • Answer one question • Spend equal time on parts (a) and (b) • 55 minutes • 40 marks	**Poetry since 1789** • Part 1: Poetry anthology: answer one question/ 35 minutes/20 marks • Part 2: Unseen poetry: answer question/ 45 minutes/20 marks	**No section C**
Eduqas	Paper 1: Shakespeare and Poetry • 2 hours • 80 marks • 40% of GCSE	**Shakespeare** • Answer a two-part question • 1 hour • 40 marks	**Poetry** • Answer a two-part question • 1 hour • 40 marks	**No section C**
	Paper 2: Post-1914 Prose/ Drama, 19th Century Prose and Unseen Poetry • 2 hours 30 minutes • 120 marks • 60% of GCSE	**Post-1914 Prose/Drama** • Answer one question • 45 minutes • 40 marks	**19th Century Prose** • Answer one question • 45 minutes • 40 marks	**Unseen Poetry** • Answer a two-part question • 1 hour • 40 marks
OCR	Paper 1: Exploring modern and literary heritage texts • 2 hours • 80 marks • 50% of GCSE	**Modern prose or drama** • Answer a two-part question • 1 hour 15 minutes • 40 marks	**19th century prose** • Answer one question • 45 minutes • 40 marks	**No section C**
	Paper 2: Exploring poetry and Shakespeare • 2 hours • 80 marks • 50% of GCSE	**Poetry across time** • Answer a two-part question • 1 hour 15 minutes • 40 marks	**Shakespeare** • Answer one question • 45 minutes • 40 marks	**No section C**

Shakespeare

Introduction and advice

You will have studied one Shakespeare play, such as:

- *Macbeth*
- *Romeo and Juliet*
- *The Tempest*
- *The Merchant of Venice*
- *Much Ado About Nothing*
- *Julius Caesar*

The exam paper will have questions on different Shakespeare plays. Don't be put off by this. You need to find the play you have studied and only answer a question on that.

On the paper you will find a short extract from the play you have studied and you will be asked to write about the extract, and about the play as a whole.

DO IT!

Set a timer for three minutes. On a large piece of paper, make a spider diagram of everything you can remember about your Shakespeare play.

Differences between the exam boards

SNAP IT! Personalise it! Shakespeare

Board			
AQA	☞ Paper 1: Section A ☞ Marks: 34 ☞ Time: 1 hour ☞ You will be assessed on AO1, AO2, AO3 and AO4.	**Eduqas**	☞ Paper 1: Section A ☞ Marks: 40 ☞ Time: 1 hour ☞ You need to answer parts (a) and (b). ☞ You will be asked to write about an aspect of the whole play that is not covered by the extract. ☞ You will be assessed on AO1, AO2 and AO4.
Edexcel	☞ Paper 1: Section A ☞ Marks: 40 ☞ Time: 55 minutes ☞ You need to answer parts (a) and (b). ☞ You will be assessed on AO1, AO2 and AO3.	**OCR**	☞ Paper 2: Section B ☞ Marks: 40 ☞ Time: 45 minutes ☞ You will get a choice of questions on your Shakespeare play. You can either write about the extract and a relevant theme in the whole play, or you can write an essay that does not use the extract at all. ☞ You will be assessed on AO1, AO2, AO3 and AO4.

The assessment objectives for English Literature are below:

AO1	Read, understand and respond to texts. Students should be able to: • maintain a critical style and develop an informed personal response • use textual references, including quotations, to support and illustrate interpretations.
AO2	Analyse the language, form and structure used by a writer to create meanings and effects, using relevant subject terminology where appropriate.
AO3	Show understanding of the relationships between texts and the contexts in which they were written.
AO4	Use a range of vocabulary and sentence structures for clarity, purpose and effect, with accurate spelling and punctuation.

NAILIT!

Remember this is a closed book exam, so you will not be able to take your text into the examination. You must be confident and familiar with the play you have studied.

Understanding the question

Although there is only one question to choose from (except OCR), you are asked to do two tasks:

1 Write in detail about a short extract from a Shakespeare play you have studied.

2 Write about the play as a whole.

The questions will ask you to look at an aspect of the play: for example, theme, character or plot development, or even a mixture of these aspects.

The question on the paper will look something like this:

Macbeth

Read the following extract from Act 5 Scene 5 of *Macbeth* and then answer the question that follows.

At this point in the play Macbeth is speaking. He has just been told that his wife, Lady Macbeth, is dead.

> She should have died hereafter.
>
> There would have been a time for such a word.
>
> Tomorrow, and tomorrow, and tomorrow,
>
> Creeps in this petty pace from day to day
>
> 5   To the last syllable of recorded time,
>
> And all our yesterdays have lighted fools
>
> The way to dusty death. Out, out, brief candle!
>
> Life's but a walking shadow, a poor player
>
> That struts and frets his hour upon the stage
>
> 10 And then is heard no more. It is a tale
>
> Told by an idiot, full of sound and fury,
>
> Signifying nothing.

Starting with this speech, explain how far you think Shakespeare presents Macbeth as a desperate and changed man.

Write about:

(a) how Shakespeare presents Macbeth in this speech

(b) how Shakespeare presents Macbeth in the play as a whole.

Using the extract

Consider the first part of the question: **how does Shakespeare present the character in the speech?** The question will be about either a theme or character in the play. When writing about the extract it is helpful to think about language, structure and subject terminology.

Looking at language means thinking about the words that Shakespeare chooses to give his character.

In the exam, you should read through the extract and pick out interesting words or short phrases, making some annotations in the margin about how language is used and its effect.

WORKIT!

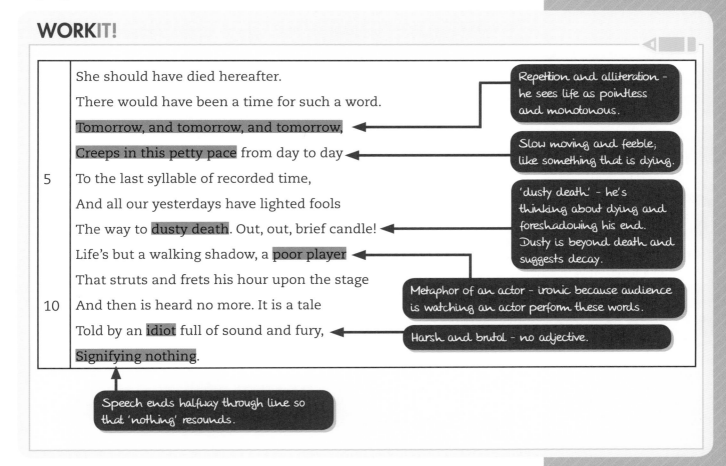

	She should have died hereafter.
	There would have been a time for such a word.
	Tomorrow, and tomorrow, and tomorrow,
	Creeps in this petty pace from day to day
5	To the last syllable of recorded time,
	And all our yesterdays have lighted fools
	The way to dusty death. Out, out, brief candle!
	Life's but a walking shadow, a poor player
	That struts and frets his hour upon the stage
10	And then is heard no more. It is a tale
	Told by an idiot full of sound and fury,
	Signifying nothing.

Repetition and alliteration – he sees life as pointless and monotonous.

Slow moving and feeble, like something that is dying.

'dusty death' – he's thinking about dying and foreshadowing his end. Dusty is beyond death and suggests decay.

Metaphor of an actor – ironic because audience is watching an actor perform these words.

Harsh and brutal – no adjective.

Speech ends halfway through line so that 'nothing' resounds.

Next, consider the structure of the extract. This means the way it is organised and put together. Use a different colour to highlight words or phrases in your chosen extract. Make some more annotations, this time about structure. Think about the position of the words and phrases in the extract – why might Shakespeare have chosen to arrange them in this way? What sort of impact on the audience is he trying to build?

Remember, you need to use subject terminology (specialist words or phrases that relate to the subject) such as metaphor, verb, image and alliteration. Write down all the specialist terms and literary techniques you can remember from your study of English Literature. Think about your work in poetry to help you. Start with rhythm, simile and onomatopoeia.

DOIT!

Using the extract on page 110, or a key extract from your Shakespeare play, mark up the text with some annotations about language and structure using the advice given.

NAILIT!

Make sure that you always explain the terminology you use and back it up with examples. 'Macbeth uses an extended metaphor' on its own will get no marks in the exam. Instead, explain why that technique has been used, and its effect on the audience (both Elizabethan and modern).

DO IT!

Pick out two or three literary techniques from the extract on page 110 or your own extract and annotate them with notes explaining why you think Shakespeare chose to use them.

DO IT!

Choose three of your annotations and write one or two sentences about each.

DO IT!

Write down five or six bullet points about the characterisation of each of the four main characters in the play you have studied. Back up each with an example from the text from the play.

WORKIT!

'dusty death' - alliteration

'life's but a poor player' - metaphor

Throughout the speech, Macbeth uses the extended metaphor of an actor on the stage. Shakespeare does this to show that, even though life might be exciting at the time, ultimately it is short and meaningless.

WORKIT!

The repetition of 'tomorrow' takes up a whole line, suggesting Shakespeare is instructing the actor to speak in a slow repetitive rhythm because Macbeth sees life as monotonous and hopeless.

Characters and relationships

Many exam questions focus on an important character – or the relationship between particular characters. This doesn't mean you have to write about **everything** the character does or says. The question will guide you towards particular moments and events and aspects of the character. You will need to choose relevant parts of the play for yourself, so you must know it well.

Of course, characters are not real people: they do not have a life of their own; instead, they are created by the playwright. How the playwright presents a character is what we call characterisation. As an English Literature student, it is really important to write about the **characters** in a way that shows you know Shakespeare has created them to perform on the stage. Don't write about them as if they are real people. Above all, you will want to think about their motivation. What is it they want? Macbeth wants power, Juliet wants to be with Romeo and escape the shackles of the life her parents have chosen.

Shakespeare's plays are always about the **relationships** between characters. In *Romeo and Juliet*, Juliet's relationship with Romeo is obviously central to the play, but her relationships with her father, mother and the nurse are also important. The relationships between characters in *Much Ado About Nothing* are complex and tangled.

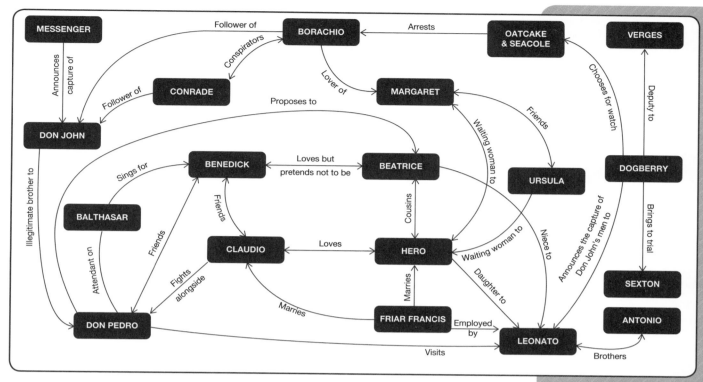

Relationship web for *Much Ado About Nothing*

Themes and motifs

A good writer ties their work together with themes – a group of ideas and images they keep referring back to, such as death, darkness, love or family.

SNAPIT!

Make a diagram like the one above to show the relationships between the central characters in the play you have studied. Then take a photograph of it so that you can revisit it anywhere!

DOIT!

1 Make a theme web. Choose a theme or motif from the play you have studied. Write the name of the theme on a piece of card and stick it to a large sheet of paper. Write events, ideas and quotations to do with that theme on pieces of card and arrange them on the paper. Put the most important events/ideas/quotations closest to the theme card. Repeat this for two or three themes.

- Macbeth – darkness.
- The murder of Duncan takes place at night.
- Just before murder of Banquo, Macbeth says, 'Nature seems dead, and wicked dreams abuse/The curtained sleep.'

2 Write a paragraph about the significance of one of your themes using ideas from your web. Make sure you back up your ideas with at least one quotation.

DOIT!

Reduce your play to the ten most important events. You could compare your ten key events with someone else. Discuss, argue and agree a combined list of ten.

DOIT!

Choose a particular scene from your play and write a sentence explaining how the setting informs what we understand about the characters.

☞ Context is not tested in the Shakespeare question.

Eduqas

☞ Context is tested only in part (b), where you write about the whole play.

Edexcel

Plot development

The plot of a play or novel is its story – its events – and how those events are ordered and manipulated by the writer for the maximum effect on the audience. For a writer, plot development is about how they gradually reveal characters and their relationships, and how the main themes are presented. Plot development is therefore about manipulating the audience. Of course, you have to know the plot of the play but be careful; simply retelling the story won't get you any credit in the exam. You will need to interpret the **events** to make an informed personal analysis of the play.

The setting

When and where the whole play or scene or speech takes place can influence the audience's response to the characters and their actions. For example, most of the action in *Macbeth* takes place in a cold, dark and rather lonely castle or a bleak and desolate 'blasted heath'. You can refer to setting when writing about the extract and the whole play.

Context

It helps our understanding if we know something about the historical, social and cultural circumstances in which the play was written and how this might have influenced Shakespeare. This is called context. Context can also refer to the location where the play or scene takes place, the genre and the way different audiences might watch and understand the play. A student here talks about witches in the context of Shakespearean times:

WORKIT!

In Shakespeare's time, many women had been executed for supposed witchcraft. This meant the audience believed the witches had genuine supernatural power.

DOIT!

Read these two responses by students who were writing about context in a Shakespeare essay.

Student answer A

Shakespeare was born in 1564 and died in 1616, his father was a glove maker and he went to a school in Stratford-Upon-Avon.

Student answer B

Juliet is very young 'she hath not seen the change of fourteen years' and yet the friar sees it as appropriate for her to be married to Romeo. However, in Shakespeare's time it was not her young age that was unsuitable but the fact that the marriage had taken place in secret.

Which do you think is best and why? Write some feedback for each student.

Mark scheme

These improvement descriptors will help you to understand how to improve your answers.

 SNAPIT!

Descriptors	Band 2	Band 3	Band 4	Band 5	Band 6
AO1 Read, understand and respond Use evidence	The student's answer… • is relevant and backs up ideas with references to the text • makes some comments about these references	The student's answer… • sometimes explains the text in relation to the task • refers to details in the text to back up points	The student's answer… • clearly explains the text in relation to the task • uses textual references effectively to back up points	The student's answer… • thoughtfully explains the text in relation to the task • thoughtfully builds appropriate references into points	The student's answer… • critically explores the text in relation to the task • chooses precise textual details to clinch points
AO2 Language, form and structure Subject terminology	• mentions some of the writer's methods • uses some subject terminology	• comments on some of the writer's methods and their effects • uses some relevant terminology	• clearly explains the writer's key methods, and their effects • helpfully uses varied, relevant terminology	• thoughtfully explains the writer's key methods, and their effects • makes thoughtful use of relevant terminology	• analyses the writer's key methods, and how these influence the reader • chooses subject terminology to make points precise and convincing
AO3 Contexts (Not Eduqas)	• makes some simple inferences and shows some awareness of contexts.	• infers the writer's point of view and the significance of contexts.	• shows a clear appreciation of the writer's point of view and the significance of contexts.	• explores the writer's point of view and the influence of particular contexts.	• makes perceptive and revealing links between the text and relevant contexts.

You can find the assessment objectives on page 109.

NAIL IT!

In the Shakespeare part of the exam you will also be tested on AO4 – your ability to use a range of vocabulary and sentence structures for clarity, purpose and effect, with accurate spelling and punctuation.

From this mark scheme you will realise that:

Very good answers will explore how Shakespeare uses language and structure to create characters and their relationships. Very good answers connect what the characters say to the themes, ideas and effects upon the reader.

Good answers will show a clear understanding of how Shakespeare develops characters and relationships, using strong examples.

Weaker answers will only explain what happens to characters and relationships without using many examples. They will write about the characters as if they are real people and not acknowledge that they are Shakespeare's constructs.

CHECK IT!

1 Choose one of these areas you have revised: characterisation, plot, settings or theme. Write a paragraph for your Shakespeare play on the area you have chosen.

2 Choose a different extract taken from the play you have studied. It should be between 15 and 20 lines (you might find it helpful to print it out). Adapt the question below to fit your chosen Shakespeare play and extract:

> Look at how [character's name] and [another character's name] speak and behave here. What does it reveal to an audience about their relationship at this point in the play? Refer closely to details from the extract to support your answer.

3 Now write about how Shakespeare presents one of those characters – or the relationship between them – at other points in the play.

The 19th-century novel

Introduction and advice

You will have studied one 19th-century novel, such as:

- *The Strange Case of Dr Jekyll and Mr Hyde* by Robert Louis Stevenson
- *A Christmas Carol* by Charles Dickens
- *Jane Eyre* by Charlotte Brontë
- *Frankenstein* by Mary Shelley
- *Pride and Prejudice* by Jane Austen
- *The War of the Worlds* by HG Wells

Differences between the exam boards

NAILIT!

Just as with the Shakespeare section, the paper will have questions on all of the novels covered by your exam board. Remember, you only need to answer the question on the novel you have studied. Once you have found your question, take some time to read through and understand it.

SNAP IT! Personalise it! 19th-century novel

Board		
AQA	☞ Paper 1: Section B ☞ Marks: 30 ☞ Time: 45 minutes ☞ You will be assessed on AO1, AO2 and AO3.	**Eduqas** ☞ Paper 2: Section B ☞ Marks: 40 ☞ Time: 45 minutes ☞ You will be assessed on AO1, AO2 and AO3.
Edexcel	☞ Paper 2: Section A ☞ Marks: 40 ☞ Time: 55 minutes ☞ You will be assessed on AO1 and AO2. ☞ You will not be tested on understanding of context.	**OCR** ☞ Paper 1: Section B ☞ Marks: 40 ☞ Time: 45 minutes ☞ You will be given a choice of questions on your 19th-century novel: you can either write about the extract and a relevant theme in the whole novel or you can write an essay that does not use the extract at all. ☞ You will be assessed on AO1, AO2, AO3 and AO4.

You can find the assessment objectives on page 109.

Understanding the question

The question will ask you to write about characters, themes, settings or a combination of these elements.

Here is a sample extract from a 19th-century novel, followed by a sample question:

Robert Louis Stevenson: *The Strange Case of Dr Jekyll and Mr Hyde*

Read this extract from Chapter 2 and then answer the following question.

In this extract Mr Utterson meets Mr Hyde.

	The steps drew swiftly nearer, and swelled out suddenly louder as they turned the end of the street. The lawyer, looking forth from the entry, could soon see what manner of man he had to deal with. He was small and very plainly dressed and the look of him, even at that distance, went somehow strongly against the watcher's inclination. But he made
5	straight for the door, crossing the roadway to save time; and as he came, he drew a key from his pocket like one approaching home.
	Mr. Utterson stepped out and touched him on the shoulder as he passed. 'Mr. Hyde, I think?'
	Mr. Hyde shrank back with a hissing intake of the breath. But his fear was only momentary; and though he did not look the lawyer in the face, he answered coolly
10	enough: 'That is my name. What do you want?'
	'I see you are going in,' returned the lawyer. 'I am an old friend of Dr. Jekyll's–Mr. Utterson of Gaunt Street–you must have heard of my name; and meeting you so conveniently, I thought you might admit me.'
	'You will not find Dr. Jekyll; he is from home,' replied Mr. Hyde, blowing in the key. And
15	then suddenly, but still without looking up, 'How did you know me?' he asked.
	'On your side,' said Mr. Utterson 'will you do me a favour?'
	'With pleasure,' replied the other. 'What shall it be?'
	'Will you let me see your face?' asked the lawyer.
	Mr. Hyde appeared to hesitate, and then, as if upon some sudden reflection, fronted about
20	with an air of defiance; and the pair stared at each other pretty fixedly for a few seconds. 'Now I shall know you again,' said Mr. Utterson. 'It may be useful.'
	'Yes,' returned Mr. Hyde, 'It is as well we have met; and apropos, you should have my address.' And he gave a number of a street in Soho.
	'Good God!' thought Mr. Utterson, 'can he, too, have been thinking of the will?' But he
25	kept his feelings to himself and only grunted in acknowledgment of the address.
	'And now,' said the other, 'how did you know me?'
	'By description,' was the reply.

Write about Mr Utterson and the impressions we get of him at different points in the novel.

In your response you should:

- **refer to the extract and the novel as a whole**

- **show your understanding of characters and events in the novel**

- **refer to the contexts of the novel.**

Using the extract

You will need to get used to dealing with extracts – short chunks of the novel. An extract is usually about 400 words long. It is helpful revision to create your own bank of likely extracts.

DO IT!

1. Start by revising an overview of the novel. Decide on the ten most important events and summarise each in one sentence. Find the event in the novel and select an extract of about 400 words. Make a copy of your chosen extract, so that you can annotate it.

2. Re-read your extract, paying close attention to how the writer uses language. As you do so, underline interesting words and phrases and make annotations in the margins. Look at the language the writer uses. These questions will help you:
   - How does the writer use language to convey the setting or mood in the extract?
   - What effect does the language have? Consider: what does it make the reader think of? How does it make them feel?
   - If the writer uses dialogue, how do they make it interesting?
   - How do different characters speak?
   - How does the writer choose words for deliberate impact?
   - Which words or phrases tell you that this extract was written in the 19th century?

3. Read your extract and write one or two sentences for each of these questions:
   - Which characters appear and how are they presented?
   - How does the writer use a range of techniques in the extract to create a particular atmosphere?
   - Write down two other places in the novel that have similar ideas, language or details.
   - Write down two themes in the extract and find two other places in the novel where those themes are used.

Thinking about the novel as a whole

As well as the extract, the question will ask you to write about the novel as a whole, so you need to understand the complete book. These review activities will help you revise for this.

DO IT!

WORKIT!

'Great Expectations' starts in a very dramatic way. Pip is alone in the churchyard; suddenly the convict, Magwitch, attacks him. Dickens makes his central character vulnerable and right away the reader wants to know what happens to him. This vulnerability is echoed when he later goes go visit Miss Haversham. He is seen to be a small boy in a huge, frightening and semi-derelict house.

Find your list of the ten key events from the first Do it! on this page. Write each event on a separate card. Then add in five more events on new cards. Shuffle them and pin them up in the right order.

Write answers to these questions on the cards.

- How do the events relate to each other?
- Why do you think the writer has structured a particular event in that place in the novel?

You can organise your revision around character and theme because the questions will focus on these areas. To write about character and theme, you will need to think about characterisation (the way the character is constructed), relationships, events, setting and context.

SNAPIT!

To help you review characterisation, make a quick sketch of each of the four most important characters in the novel. Annotate each sketch with seven things you know about that character. Support them with quotes that you have learned. You can then take a picture of the sketches so you can look at them whenever you want!

Here is an example, with two examples of characterisation added:

Utterson in Jekyll and Hyde

→ Seems dreary but 'somehow lovable'.

→ Cold and embarrassed.

DOIT!

Make a table, like the one shown below, for the 19th-century novel you are studying.

In your chosen 19th-century novel, the writer will keep returning to central ideas (or themes), such as loneliness, growing up or the danger of unrestrained science. It is helpful to connect these themes to specific and concrete events in the novel.

WORKIT!

Frankenstein			
Theme	Event	Quotation	How does this make the theme concrete?
Exploration	Walton's ship is freed from the ice and he returns home.	'It is past: I am returning to England. I have lost my hopes of utility and glory.'	Walton believes that his expedition has been a failure but he has not made the same mistakes as Frankenstein in pursuing his dream.
Creation			
Family			
The monstrous and the human			

Here is an example of an answer based on *A Christmas Carol*:

WORKIT!

The language that Scrooge uses when he sees his younger self in the schoolroom juxtaposes with the language he uses when his nephew visits at the beginning of the novella.

'Why, it's Ali Baba!' Scrooge exclaimed in ecstasy. 'It's dear old honest Ali Baba! Yes, yes, I know.' Here he is enthusiastic and excited, as if he is a young boy again. This is significant because...

DO IT!

Look at the questions about language when you focused on the extract in the previous section (page 119). Connect this to the novel as a whole. Find two places in the novel where language is used in a similar way, and find two places in the novel where language is used in a very different way.

03 Context

Even if your understanding of context is not being tested directly, your understanding (and enjoyment) of the novel is greatly improved if you have some understanding of its context. It helps our understanding if we know something about the circumstances in which the novel was written and how this might have influenced the writer. Context can also refer to the location where the novel or scene takes place, the genre and the way different readers might understand the novel. For example, how does the context of the time in which you live influence your understanding of the novel?

Here is an example for Mary Shelley's *Frankenstein*:

NAILIT!

Remember that Edexcel does not test understanding of context in the 19th-century novel question.

WORKIT!

In the early 19th century, people were fascinated by science and its possibilities. Mary Shelley explores this theme in her novel 'Frankenstein'. The novel becomes a warning about where uncontrolled science might lead.

DO IT!

Use the internet or notes from your studies to research three things that were important at the time your chosen 19th-century novel was written. Write two or three sentences explaining how these ideas and attitudes might have influenced the writer.

Setting

The setting of the novel as a whole, or an individual scene, can help create tone and atmosphere. Setting tends to refer to the place or places in which the novel takes place. The setting can influence the reader's response to the characters, their actions and the themes.

WORKIT!

A Christmas Carol					
	Setting	**Event**	**Chapter**	**Quotation**	**How is the setting used?**
1	Scrooge's counting house on Christmas Eve.	Scrooge's nephew visits to wish him 'Merry Christmas'.	(Stave) 1	'Scrooge had a very small fire, but the clerk's fire was so very much smaller that it looked like one coal.'	Scrooge is miserable and mean. Cold and unwelcoming. Opposite to the way Christmas should be.
2					
3					
4					

DOIT!

Create a table like the one shown above to identify four key settings in the 19th-century novel you have studied.

Mark scheme

The exam marker will use a mark scheme like the one used for the Shakespeare paper (see page 115).

Very good answers will explore the writer's craft. They will connect what the characters do and their relationships. They will explore how the writer communicates their ideas to the reader. They will give a personal response. They will use examples and quotations and explain them.

Good answers will show a clear understanding and use well-chosen examples.

Weaker answers will retell the story. They won't use examples to show knowledge of the novel and they won't say anything about the writer's craft.

NAILIT!

OCR is the only exam board that will give some marks for vocabulary, spelling, sentence structures and punctuation (AO4) on this part of the exam.

CHECKIT!

1 How many minutes should you leave to do the 19th-century novel question?

2 How long is the given extract likely to be?

3 What is meant by 'theme', and what are the central themes in the novel you have studied?

Modern texts

Introduction and advice

You will have studied one modern novel or play such as:

- *An Inspector Calls* by JB Priestley
- *Blood Brothers* by Willy Russell
- *The Woman in Black* by Susan Hill
- *The Curious Incident of the Dog in the Night-Time* by Simon Stephens
- *Lord of the Flies* by William Golding
- *Never Let Me Go* by Kazuo Ishiguro
- *Anita and Me* by Meera Syal

When you have found the questions about your play/novel they will look something like the ones below. Remember, you only have to choose one question to answer.

JB Priestley: *An Inspector Calls*

EXAMPLE 1

Birling: *I've got to cover this up as soon as I can.*

Explore how respectability is important in the play.

You must refer to the context of the play in your answer.

EXAMPLE 2

How does Priestley use Eva Smith in *An Inspector Calls* to explore ideas about social responsibility?

NAILIT!

The paper will feature questions on all the books that could have been chosen for study – not just yours. You only need to answer the question on your novel or play. Once you have found the question on your text, take some time to read through and understand it.

NAILIT!

Remember this is a closed book exam, so you will not be able to take your text into the examination. You must be confident and familiar with the text you have studied.

NAILIT!

Remember to make notes while you're re-reading your chosen text – these can be in the form of tables, annotations, drawings and key quotes. This will help to keep your mind active.

Differences between the exam boards

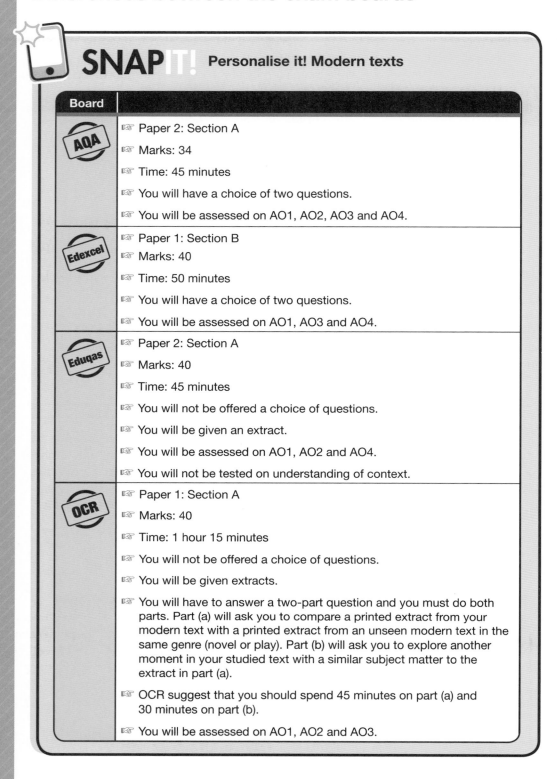

SNAP IT! Personalise it! Modern texts

Board	
AQA	☞ Paper 2: Section A ☞ Marks: 34 ☞ Time: 45 minutes ☞ You will have a choice of two questions. ☞ You will be assessed on AO1, AO2, AO3 and AO4.
Edexcel	☞ Paper 1: Section B ☞ Marks: 40 ☞ Time: 50 minutes ☞ You will have a choice of two questions. ☞ You will be assessed on AO1, AO3 and AO4.
Eduqas	☞ Paper 2: Section A ☞ Marks: 40 ☞ Time: 45 minutes ☞ You will not be offered a choice of questions. ☞ You will be given an extract. ☞ You will be assessed on AO1, AO2 and AO4. ☞ You will not be tested on understanding of context.
OCR	☞ Paper 1: Section A ☞ Marks: 40 ☞ Time: 1 hour 15 minutes ☞ You will not be offered a choice of questions. ☞ You will be given extracts. ☞ You will have to answer a two-part question and you must do both parts. Part (a) will ask you to compare a printed extract from your modern text with a printed extract from an unseen modern text in the same genre (novel or play). Part (b) will ask you to explore another moment in your studied text with a similar subject matter to the extract in part (a). ☞ OCR suggest that you should spend 45 minutes on part (a) and 30 minutes on part (b). ☞ You will be assessed on AO1, AO2 and AO3.

You can find the assessment objectives on page 109.

Plot: the story and structure of the text

Although you won't be asked a question directly about the plot, it is important to know what happens. You will need to be able to recall different events and sequences from the novel or play and to write about them in some detail.

DOIT!

1 Give yourself ten minutes to draw a storyboard of the novel. Stick people will do! A storyboard is a collection of drawings based on the main events of the novel.
2 When you have finished, reduce the play/novel to the ten most important quotations. Write them on sticky notes and stick them on the wall in the order they happen.
3 Look at the storyboard and quotes regularly, and familiarise yourself with them over a number of days.

Here is the start of a list of quotations for *Lord of the Flies*:

WORKIT!

- 'Within the diamond haze of the beach something dark was fumbling along.'

- 'Startled, Ralph realized that the boys were falling still and silent, feeling the beginnings of awe at the power set free below them. The knowledge and awe made him savage.'

SNAPIT!

Make profiles for **four of the main** characters in your play or novel. Start by making a quick sketch, paying attention to facial expressions and clothing. Then annotate the sketch with seven things you know about the character. Add at least one quotation to each character profile. You can then take a picture of these profiles so that you can revisit them easily, wherever you are!
Here is an unfinished example of a profile for Mr Birling from *An Inspector Calls*.

At start of play he is pompous and arrogant.

He calls Eva Smith 'a wretched girl' and is not interested in her suicide.

He thinks he will be given a knighthood.

He believes it would be impossible to be responsible for all our actions.

DOIT!

Choose one of the characters and write down four questions you would ask them to probe their attitudes. Find someone to work with and role play the character. Alternatively, write answers to the questions in the first person (as if you are the character).

Themes

DO IT!

Make a themes grid for the modern text you have studied, like the one below, and complete it.

A theme is a set of ideas, which the writer examines in their work. They return to the theme at different moments. For example, in *The Curious Incident of the Dog in the Night-Time*, Simon Stephens explores themes of isolation, fear, love and identity amongst others. In *An Inspector Calls*, Priestley explores themes of social responsibility, hypocrisy and snobbery.

WORKIT!

An Inspector Calls			
Theme	**Event**	**Supporting quotation**	**How this refers to the theme**
Lies and secrecy	Gerald says he saved Eva at the palace bar from Alderman Joe Meggarty.	'The girl... gave me a glance that was nothing less than a cry for help.'	He hasn't told Sheila anything about his relationship with Eva until now.
Differences between generations			
Social class and snobbery			
Social responsibility			

The exam question below could easily be adapted to suit the modern text you have studied. Think about how you might plan an answer for your own text.

Write about how [name of author/playwright] explores the theme of [name of theme] in [name of play/novel].

Language

The language the writer uses is vitally important in conveying the meaning in their text. The author's voice might be complex or straightforward. They may be honest with their reader or writing to confuse or trick them. Their tone may be serious or comical.

A writer will often choose to tell a particular part of the story from the point of view of a particular character. Here is an extract from *Lord of the Flies*:

> Ralph wept for the end of innocence, the darkness of man's heart, and the fall through the air of a true, wise friend called Piggy.

Although Golding is writing about Ralph in the third person, he is clearly looking at Ralph's feelings and exploring these ideas from Ralph's point of view.

A writer will use language to create the mood and atmosphere and to control how we react to characters and events. For example, one student wrote:

WORKIT!

In Chapter 12 of 'Lord of the Flies', when 'Ralph launched himself like a cat; stabbed, snarling, with the spear, and the savage doubled up', the quick, sharp language creates the sense of a chase. The alliteration of the 's' sounds and the frequent use of commas make the atmosphere fast, exciting and breathless.

This student has focused on language and analyses the way the author creates the atmosphere by examining some of the methods Golding uses.

Of course, the dialogue the characters use and the way they say it reveals much about them.

When questioned by the Inspector in *An Inspector Calls*, Mrs Birling says:

'And if you'd take some steps to find this young man and then make sure that he's compelled to confess in public his responsibility – instead of staying here asking quite unnecessary questions – then you really would be doing your duty.'

She assumes the higher status and tells the inspector how to do his job. Her choice of language reveals her arrogant attitude and shows how out of touch she is with events.

The language of a play

If you are studying a play you will need to remember that the form means the writer has to use slightly different tools. They cannot use long passages of narration to get across their message. However, they can use stage directions. These are chosen precisely and often reveal important aspects of character.

Below is what one student wrote about the stage directions at the beginning of *An Inspector Calls*.

WORKIT!

The stage directions at the start of 'An Inspector Calls' tell us that Arthur Birling is in 'evening dress' and 'white tie'. This suggests to the audience that he is wealthy. Priestley says that he is 'provincial in his speech' suggesting that Birling has risen to wealth from a modest background.

Here, the student identifies what the playwright says but goes on to explain the meaning behind it.

DO IT!

When analysing language you need to look at short quotations in detail. Choose three quotations from the beginning, middle and end of the modern prose or drama you have studied. Write them down. Make notes on each under these headings:

- Author's voice
- Point of view
- Mood and atmosphere
- Attitude
- Stage directions (if you have studied a play)

Here is an example of a quote that a student picked from Chapter 6 of *Lord of the Flies* and their notes about it.

WORKIT!

> Even the sounds of nightmare from the other shelters no longer reached him, for he was back to where he came from, feeding the ponies with sugar over the garden wall.

- Author's voice – straightforward and authoritative, like the narrator of a boys' adventure story.
- Point of view – Ralph.
- Mood and atmosphere – words like nightmare at the start of the sentence tell us how horrible the situation is but this is juxtaposed with the sweetness of 'sugar' and the pleasant, safe and peaceful image of the garden.
- Attitude – Ralph seems to be showing a strong attitude where he can detach himself from the horrors of the island.

Remember to write about individual words or sentence structure and their effects (what they make the reader think of, and how they make them feel).

For example, look at this student's answer about *The Curious Incident of the Dog in the Night-Time*:

WORKIT!

> I do not like people shouting at me. It makes me scared that they are going to hit me or touch me and I do not know what is going to happen.

Christopher uses simple sentences with no commas. He repeats 'do not' making it very clear what he thinks.

Setting

The setting of a play or novel refers to the time and place of the story. The writer uses setting to establish the background, mood and atmosphere of the action. Here is an example of a student writing about the setting at the beginning of *An Inspector Calls*:

WORKIT!

> It has good solid furniture of the period. The general effect is substantial and heavily comfortable, but not cosy and homelike.

At the opening of the play the audience sees the dining room of a large suburban house. Immediately, we know that this is a well-off family who seem apparently comfortable and content. Priestley presents carefully chosen details to suggest that the family is awkward and there will be difficulties ahead. For example:

Context

A novel or play may have many contexts. Any line or sentence fits into the context of the whole work. The work is influenced by the context in which it was written. Understanding the context gives you greater understanding and insight. As an English Literature student, you will be expected to show some of these insights in the exam.

Answer these questions to help you think about the context of your modern text:

- When was it written?
- Who was the original audience?
- What ideas and issues do you think the writer was trying to explore in the play/novel?
- What would the reader/audience have thought about these ideas?
- What does the novel/play have to say to us today and why is this relevant?

Quotations

Quotations can be an important and useful form of evidence to back up your ideas. They show that you have a good in-depth knowledge of your modern text. It is worth choosing some key quotations and learning them.

Choose one setting from your modern play/prose and draw a map or plan of it. Use quotations and supporting evidence from your chosen text to annotate it. Then choose four details from your map or plan and write a paragraph about each, explaining what this detail tells the audience/reader. Include a key quote for each one.

NAILIT!

Remember, Eduqas does not test understanding of context in the modern text question.

Here are two useful quotations from *Lord of the Flies*:

- Jack and Ralph look at each other 'baffled, in love and hate'.
- Simon suddenly gets in his mind a 'picture of a human at once heroic and sick'.

Now look at how these quotations have been used in two different student answers:

DOIT!

1 Decide on five or more key quotations in your play/novel. Try to limit your choice to quotations of no more than seven words. Think about the different ways that you can use the quotations. It may be possible to use the same quotation to make a point about character, setting or language.

2 Write the quotations on separate cards. Carry them around with you and learn them over a period of time.

3 Test yourself on whether you can remember the quotations without looking at them.

4 Try writing about your modern text, using the quotations.

WORKIT!

Student answer A

The tragedy of the boys' time on the island is that it could have turned out differently. Jack and Ralph are the key characters and they have mixed feelings about each other: early on they were 'baffled, in love and hate'. This shows that they could have worked very closely together under different circumstances. Simon too recognises the contradictions in people – how they can be very good or very bad. He suddenly gets a mental 'picture of a human at once heroic and sick'. In other words, we have the potential for evil or goodness.

Student answer B

'Baffled, in love and hate', Jack and Ralph nearly become close friends and collaborators for the good of all the boys, but, unfortunately, through a combination of circumstances, mutual misunderstanding leads to mutual hatred and then tragedy is inevitable. Simon recognises this tragic contradiction when he suddenly realises that humans are both 'heroic and sick' at the same time. The word 'sick' implies that humans aren't really to blame: they can't control themselves and stay good and rational.

Both of these answers are very good. However, the student in version B integrates quotations with their arguments, and integrating quotations gives their arguments fluency, and – more importantly – satisfies the mark scheme descriptors for the highest grades.

Preparing for the exam

Now that you have revised what you know about your novel/play, you need to practise applying these skills and knowledge under pressure. Detailed essay plans, timed essay plans and timed essays are the best way to do this.

You can make up your own exam-style questions by adapting the ones below.

> Do you think [name of character] is an important character in [name of modern play/novel]? Write about:
> - how [name of writer] presents the character
> - how [name of writer] uses [name of character] to present ideas about people and society.

If you were studying *Lord of the Flies*, this question could become:

> Do you think Piggy is an important character in *Lord of the Flies*? Write about:
> - how Golding presents the character of Piggy
> - how Golding uses Piggy to present ideas about people and society.

> How and why does [name of character] change in [name of modern play/novel]?
>
> Write about:
> - how [name of character] responds to other characters
> - how [name of writer] presents [name of character] by the way they write.

> How does [name of writer] explore [theme] in [name of modern play/novel]?
>
> Write about:
> - the ideas about [name of theme] in [name of modern play/novel]
> - how [name of writer] presents these ideas in the way they write.

 STRETCHIT!

Try to integrate some quotations into your points if you are going for the highest grades.

Detailed essay plans can be notes, lists or spider diagrams. Detailed essay plans allow you to think around the subject without worrying too much about writing at this stage in your revision.

In the exam, you will only have about five minutes to make your essay plan. It is very important that you get quick and efficient at this. You'll find that the more you do, the better you get. You can often recycle ideas from one plan to another.

Mark scheme

The exam marker will be using a mark scheme like this to help grade your work:

SNAPIT!

Descriptors	Band 2	Band 3	Band 4	Band 5	Band 6
AO1 Read, understand and respond Use evidence	The student's answer… • is relevant and backs up ideas with references to the text • makes some comments about these references	The student's answer… • often explains the text in relation to the task • uses references to support a range of relevant comments	The student's answer… • clearly explains the text in relation to the task • uses references effectively to support explanations	The student's answer… • thoughtfully explains the text in relation to the task • uses references which are integrated into the answer	The student's answer… • critically explains the text in relation to the task • uses references which are judiciously integrated into the answer
AO2 Language, form and structure Subject terminology	• identifies the writer's methods • makes some reference to subject terminology	• comments on the writer's methods, and the effects these have on the reader • uses some relevant terminology	• clearly explains the writer's methods, and the effects these have on the reader • makes apt use of relevant terminology	• effectively explains the writer's methods, and the effects these have on the reader • makes effective use of relevant terminology	• judiciously explains the writer's methods, and the effects these have on the reader • makes judicious use of relevant terminology
AO3 Contexts (not Eduqas)	• has some awareness of ideas and contexts.	• shows some understanding of the significance of contexts.	• shows a clear understanding of the significance of specific contexts.	• shows a thoughtful consideration of the significance of specific contexts.	• shows a critical consideration of the significance of specific contexts.

NAILIT!

Don't forget AO4. It is important to get those few extra marks!

The best answers will explore and evaluate what happens in the play/novel and the writer's purpose. They will use relevant quotations to analyse language, structure and the writer's meaning, using subject specific terminology. They will show a detailed understanding of the context of the play and they will use a range of vocabulary with good spelling and punctuation.

Weaker answers will tend to retell what happens and use no evidence to back up their ideas. They will have little understanding of the context of the play/novel and will show little understanding that this is a story made up and crafted by a writer.

NAILIT!

- You should spend about 45/50 minutes on Modern prose or drama (1 hour 15 mins if you are doing the OCR exam).
- Stay calm at the beginning of the exam. Take some time to find your question and read it carefully. Make sure you understand what you are being asked to do.
- Spend a few minutes making a plan and make sure the examiner can see this. You won't get marks for this but it will show that you have thought through your answer. The plan could be a spider diagram and doesn't need to be neat and tidy.
- Remember to use quotations as evidence.
- Allow yourself four minutes to check over your answer.

✓ CHECKIT!

1 Choose one of the questions you have adapted and spend 15 to 20 minutes writing a detailed essay plan. Remember, this is for revision only. In the exam you should spend only five minutes on your plan.

2 When you have finished the essay plan, write answers to these questions about your novel or play:

- What do you know about the characters, events, ideas, themes and structure? (AO1)

- What can you say about how the writer uses language and structure to get across their meaning? (AO2)

- What do you understand about the context of the play/novel and how this is relevant? (AO3)

- Which examples and quotations can you use as evidence?

3 Choose another one of your adapted questions and give yourself 5 minutes to do an exam-style essay plan.

Poetry anthology

DO IT!

Find sample exam question papers on your exam board website. Look closely at:

- where the anthology question will appear in the paper
- the typical style of the questions.

Introduction and advice

You will have studied a cluster of poems in the exam board anthology. They are from different times in history.

The question will ask you to compare two poems, only one of which will be printed on the paper. You will have to choose the other poem from your previous study in class of a relevant poem in the cluster. The question might be in two parts, but you will not have a choice of questions.

Differences between the exam boards

SNAP IT! Personalise it! Poetry anthology

Board	
AQA	☞ Paper 2: Section B ☞ Marks: 30 ☞ Time: 45 minutes ☞ You will be assessed on AO1, AO2 and AO3.
Edexcel	☞ Paper 2: Section B: Part 1 ☞ Marks: 20 ☞ Time: 35 minutes ☞ You will be assessed on AO2 and AO3.
Eduqas	☞ Paper 1: Section B ☞ Marks: 40 ☞ Time: 1 hour ☞ You should spend 20 minutes on part (a) and 40 minutes on part (b). ☞ You will be assessed on AO1, AO2 and AO3.
OCR	☞ Paper 2: Section A ☞ Marks: 40 (20 marks per part) ☞ Time: 1 hour 15 minutes ☞ You should spend 45 minutes on part (a) and 30 minutes on part (b). ☞ OCR has combined its anthology question with the unseen poem question, asking you to start by comparing an unseen poem with a poem of their choice from the anthology cluster of poems. Then you will be asked to choose another anthology poem to write about on its own. ☞ You will not be asked to comment on the significance of context. ☞ You will be assessed on AO1 and AO2.

You can find the assessment objectives on page 109.

Poems		Star rating
Percy Bysshe Shelley	Ozymandias	★
William Blake	London	★★★
William Wordsworth	The Prelude: Stealing the Boat	★★★
Robert Browning	My Last Duchess	★★
Alfred, Lord Tennyson	The Charge of the Light Brigade	★
Wilfred Owen	Exposure	★★★
Seamus Heaney	Storm on the Island	★
Ted Hughes	Bayonet Charge	★★★
Simon Armitage	Remains	★★
Jane Weir	Poppies	★★★
Carol Ann Duffy	War Photographer	★
Imtiaz Dharker	Tissue	★
Carol Rumens	The Émigrée	★
Beatrice Garland	Kamikaze	★
John Agard	Checking Out Me History	★

DO IT!

Make a list of all the poems in the cluster you have studied. Give each poem a star rating where:

*** means you feel very confident about the poem

** means you feel reasonably clear about the poem

* means you feel very unsure about the poem.

You need to know all the poems in your cluster very well, so start by revising the poems you have marked as one star. It is helpful to remind yourself of the following categories.

Meaning: making sense of the poems

As you re-read each poem, underline any words or phrases that you don't understand. If you are able, discuss them with someone else; otherwise look them up. Write two sentences to summarise your understanding of the poem.

For example, one student wrote:

WORKIT!

'Ozymandias'

Shelley retells the story of a traveller who saw a fallen statue, lying broken in the sand. It leads him to think about how all our great ideas and endeavours come to ruin.

NAILIT!

As you revise a poem, ask yourself which other poem(s) in the cluster it is like in some way. Think about:

- theme/ideas
- form and structure
- language
- imagery
- poet's perspective.

This will help you to compare poems.

NAILIT!

Make notes about the rhyme scheme and the rhythm of the poem. Decide if the poem is regular or irregular or perhaps a mixture of both.

DOIT!

1 Write a paragraph interpreting the structure in one of the poems you have worked on.
2 To help you, begin by writing down the number of stanzas (verses). Count the number of lines in each stanza and work out the line lengths by quickly counting syllables. Make a note of your results.

DOIT!

Write a paragraph explaining the imagery used in one of the poems you are revising.

Structure

Look at the way the poem is built and gather some information about structure.

Common structural features are helpful to know, but on their own they won't get you any credit. You need to interpret these structural devices and explain **why** the poet might have chosen to use them in this way. For example:

WORKIT!

'Neutral Tones'

The four even stanzas, together with the regular rhythm and the balanced ABBA rhyme scheme, make 'Neutral Tones' a very controlled poem. And yet, Hardy is writing about the heart-breaking emotions of a failed relationship. It is as if he is trying to control those emotions by giving the poem a very strict structure.

Imagery

Poetry is about engaging the reader's senses and emotions. Poets often use imagery to do this. Imagery in a poem refers to the techniques the poet uses to spark the senses. The most obvious of these is visual. However, a poem will often also engage the senses of hearing, touch, taste and smell.

When working on your poems, write down or highlight where the poet engages the senses. You could use a different colour to highlight each sense. Add some annotations to explain **why** you think the poet has done this.

Below is an example of a student's paragraph explaining imagery:

WORKIT!

'Storm on the Island'

In 'Storm on the Island', Heaney uses storm imagery to call upon our senses of hearing and touch. 'So that you can listen to the thing you fear/ Forgetting that it pummels your house too.' All of our senses are immersed in the storm, so we are not just readers or observers but experiencing it through the senses of sound and touch.

Language

Writing successfully about language is often about looking at individual words.

WORKIT!

'Exposure'

Owen describes the, 'agonies of men among its brambles'.

The word bramble is harsh and awkward to say, it seems to
echo the pain and torment the men are suffering.

> **DOIT!**
>
> Choose a poem and highlight any interesting or notable words or groups of words. Of course, once you have done this you will need to explain **why** you think the poet chooses to use these particular words.

A poet may use language in specific ways through, for example, simile, metaphor, personification, onomatopoeia and alliteration. As a literature student, it is important to understand how to use this terminology. These techniques are tools that the poet uses in their work (that's a metaphor). By using this terminology, you will show that you know the tricks of the trade (and that's alliteration).

> **DOIT!**
>
> Make a list of the poetic terms you are familiar with and write down what they mean.

WORKIT!

Simile: a comparison that uses 'as' or 'like'.

> **DOIT!**
>
> For three of the terms in your list, write a short paragraph explaining why the poet has used each.

WORKIT!

'Exposure'

Owen uses the metaphor of the 'iced east winds that
knive us'. The verb 'knive' makes the winds hostile,
vicious and violent. Owen makes us experience the war,
danger and death all around the men.

NAILIT!

Take care when using terminology. Many students think it is enough to simply identify the technique but 'Hardy uses a metaphor' will get no credit. You must explain **why** Hardy uses that metaphor – what effect does it have on the reader, and what point about love and relationships was Hardy trying to make?

Themes

A poet will want to explore themes and ideas in the poem: a set of ideas, which they keep returning to. The poems in your cluster will have themes common to many of the poems. You may have grouped them according to theme when you first looked at them in your study.

'Follower' by Seamus Heaney		
Theme	**Quotation**	**Analysis**
Growing up	'I stumbled in his hob-nailed wake.'	The child is trying to catch up. The boots seem big and almost threatening because the boy is so small.
Admiration	'An expert.'	As a boy, Heaney sees his father as perfect. There is no need for adjectives to describe him. The full stop is enough.
Identity	'I wanted to grow up and plough.'	There is a sense of longing and loss. The poet was unable to come up to his father's standards.

DOIT!

Make a themes grid like the one here for four of your three-star poems.

The viewpoint and attitude of the poet

Think about the persona (the character) who is speaking the poem. In 'Exposure', Owen writes as if he is actually at the battlefront. In 'Follower', Heaney is remembering back to his childhood.

DOIT!

Write down the viewpoint of each of your chosen poems. Write a sentence to explain the attitude in each.

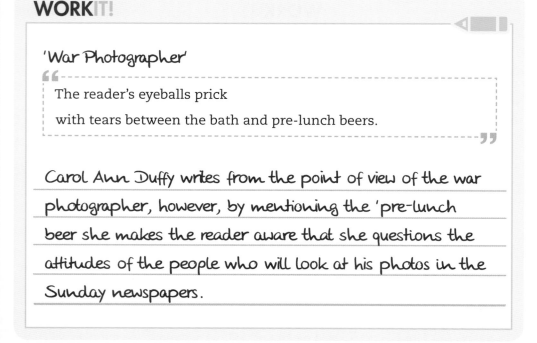

WORKIT!

'War Photographer'

> The reader's eyeballs prick
>
> with tears between the bath and pre-lunch beers.

Carol Ann Duffy writes from the point of view of the war photographer, however, by mentioning the 'pre-lunch beer she makes the reader aware that she questions the attitudes of the people who will look at his photos in the Sunday newspapers.

Context

Your understanding (and enjoyment) of the poem is greatly improved if you have some understanding of its context. Use these questions to help you think about the context of the poem you are studying.

a What do you know about the poet and their background?

b When was the poem written and how might the social and historical events of the day have influenced the poet?

Don't just mention a text's context. Only mention an aspect of context if it will deepen our understanding of the text. For example, one student wrote:

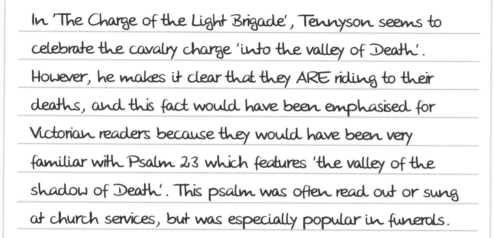

NAILIT!

Remember, OCR does not test understanding of context in the poetry anthology question.

Getting to know the poems

Once you feel comfortable that you understand the poems, use these ideas to get to know them. Remember, you will need to be able to write about them from memory.

- Test yourself by making a spider diagram of all you know about a poem. Time yourself for four minutes.

- Draw the poem as a picture or a diagram.

- Record a reading of the poem and listen to it.

- Annotate copies of the poems and display them where you can see them regularly.

- Consider how the poems in your cluster are similar/different. Draw a table or a Venn diagram to show this.

- Make a grid like the one below, putting all your thoughts about the poems in one place.

Poem	Making sense	Structure	Imagery	Language	Themes	Viewpoint and attitude
'When We Two Parted'						

Mark scheme

The exam marker will be using a mark scheme like this to help grade your work:

SNAPIT!

Descriptors	Band 2	Band 3	Band 4	Band 5	Band 6
AO1 Read, understand and compare	The student's answer… • compares texts	The student's answer… • sometimes explains valid comparisons	The student's answer… • makes clear comparisons between texts	The student's answer… • makes thoughtful, detailed comparisons between texts	The student's answer… • critically explores comparisons between texts
Use evidence	• refers to evidence and comments on it	• refers to details in the text to back up points	• uses textual references effectively to back up points	• thoughtfully builds appropriate references into points	• chooses precise textual details to clinch points
AO2 Language, form and structure	• mentions some of the writer's methods	• comments on some of the writer's methods and their effects	• clearly explains the writer's key methods, and their effects	• thoughtfully explains the writer's key methods, and their effects	• analyses the writer's key methods, and how these influence the reader
Subject terminology	• uses some subject terminology	• uses some relevant terminology	• helpfully uses varied, relevant terminology	• makes thoughtful use of relevant terminology	• chooses subject terminology to make points precise and convincing
AO3 Contexts (not OCR)	• makes some simple inferences and shows some awareness of contexts.	• infers the writer's point of view and the significance of contexts.	• shows a clear appreciation of the writer's point of view and the significance of contexts.	• explores the writer's point of view and the influence of particular contexts.	• makes perceptive and revealing links between the text and relevant contexts.

DOIT!

Look back over essays you have written about poems during your GCSE course. See if you can find examples of descriptors from the mark scheme in your answers. Set yourself some targets for improvement in your weaker areas. Make sure those targets are led by relevant descriptors in the mark scheme.

Writing about the poems in the exam

One of the poems from your anthology cluster will be printed on the exam paper. For example:

Neutral Tones

We stood by a pond that winter day,

And the sun was white, as though chidden of God,

And a few leaves lay on the starving sod;

– They had fallen from an ash, and were gray.

5 Your eyes on me were as eyes that rove

Over tedious riddles of years ago;

And some words played between us to and fro

On which lost the more by our love.

The smile on your mouth was the deadest thing

10 Alive enough to have strength to die;

And a grin of bitterness swept thereby

Like an ominous bird a-wing...

Since then, keen lessons that love deceives,

And wrings with wrong, have shaped to me

15 Your face, and the God curst sun, and a tree,

And a pond edged with grayish leaves.

Thomas Hardy

NAIL IT!

Remember, you are only allowed a copy of the first poem to look at. You must write about your chosen poem from memory.

The question about the anthology will be like one of these:

Compare the presentation of love in your chosen poem to the presentation of love in 'Neutral Tones'.

or

(a) In this poem Hardy explores ideas about love. Write about the ways in which Hardy presents love in 'Neutral Tones'.

(b) Choose one other poem from the anthology in which the poet also writes about love.

NAIL IT!

It is important you check the official exam papers produced by your exam board to find out the exact wording of the poetry anthology question.

Approach the poetry anthology question using the following steps:

1 Read through the poem on the question paper. It will be one from the cluster you have studied.

2 Decide on the poem that you will compare it with.

3 Take five minutes to annotate the printed poem. You are allowed to write on the question paper. Highlight words and phrases that are relevant to the question.

④ Use the 'Making sense of the poem – structure – imagery – language – themes – viewpoint and attitude' method from your revision to help you.

⑤ As you annotate, think about the differences and the similarities between the 'given poem' and your 'chosen poem'. Make some quick notes as annotations around the poem.

⑥ Spend a minute or so making a very quick and simple plan. This could be a spider diagram, a list or a two-column table.

⑦ Use your annotations and plan to answer the question.

⑧ Allow yourself some time to check through your answer.

It is generally more straightforward to compare the poems as you go. Don't write everything about the 'given poem' first and then start writing about your 'chosen poem'. Constantly compare the two poems through your essay to examine their similarities and differences.

Show that you can refer to details in the text by quoting from the poem printed on the exam paper. Make sure your quotations are relevant and useful.

DOIT!

1 Use your themes grid (from Do it! on page 138) to help you adapt one of the questions below to suit two poems in your poetry cluster. For example:

(a) Write about the ways in which [poet's name] presents love in [title of poem].

(b) Choose one other poem from the anthology in which the poet also writes about love.

OR

Compare the presentation of love in your chosen poem to the presentation of love in [name of poem].

OR

Compare how poets present attitudes towards [name of theme] in [name of poem] and in one other poem from your poetry cluster.

2 Make a detailed essay plan in answer to your question. Use your revision notes to help you think about:
- making sense of the poem
- its structure
- its imagery
- its language
- its themes
- the poet's viewpoint and attitude.

CHECKIT! ✓

1 Name one particularly successful focus when writing about language.

2 Name the only good reason for writing about context.

3 How many poems will the question ask you to compare?

Unseen poetry

Introduction and advice

You will be given two poems to write about. These will not be poems you have studied before. It is not possible to predict which poems the exam board will choose.

Differences between the exam boards

SNAP IT! Personalise it! Unseen poetry

Board	
AQA	☞ Paper 2: Section C ☞ Marks: 32 ☞ Time: 45 minutes ☞ You will be asked to write about one poem and then compare it with the second poem. ☞ You will be assessed on AO1 and AO2.
Edexcel	☞ Paper 2: Section B: Part 2 ☞ Marks: 20 ☞ Time: 45 minutes ☞ You will be asked to compare an aspect of the two poems. ☞ You will be assessed on AO1 and AO2.
Eduqas	☞ Paper 2: Section C ☞ Marks: 40 ☞ Time: 1 hour ☞ You will be asked to write about one poem and then compare it with the second poem. ☞ You will be assessed on AO1 and AO2.
OCR	☞ Paper 2: Section A ☞ Marks: 40 (20 marks per part) ☞ Time: 1 hour 15 minutes ☞ You should spend 45 minutes on part (a) and 30 minutes on part (b). ☞ OCR has combined its anthology question with the unseen poem, asking you to start by comparing an unseen poem with a poem of their choice from the anthology cluster of poems. ☞ You will be assessed on AO1 and AO2.

You can find the assessment objectives on page 109.

DO IT!

Make a list of all the skills you have learned to help you analyse a poem.

Revising for the unseen poems

It is unlikely that you will have seen the poem on the exam paper before. Revision for this section is about practising the skills you have learned and using them quickly and accurately.

Use the skills you have developed when studying the anthology (see pages 134–42) to analyse the unseen poems. Much of the revision in this will help you prepare for writing about the unseen poems.

The first unseen poem

Read this example of an unseen poem:

Catrin

I can remember you, child,
As I stood in a hot, white
Room at the window watching
The people and cars taking
5   Turn at the traffic lights.
I can remember you, our first
Fierce confrontation, the tight
Red rope of love which we both
Fought over. It was a square
10   Environmental blank, disinfected
Of paintings or toys. I wrote
All over the walls with my
Words, coloured the clean squares
With the wild, tender circles
15   Of our struggle to become
Separate. We want, we shouted,
To be two, to be ourselves.

Neither won nor lost the struggle
In the glass tank clouded with feelings
20   Which changed us both. Still I am fighting
You off, as you stand there
With your straight, strong, long
Brown hair and your rosy,
Defiant glare, bringing up
25   From the heart's pool that old rope,
Tightening about my life,
Trailing love and conflict,
As you ask may you skate
In the dark, for one more hour.

Gillian Clarke

Making sense of the poem

1 Read Gillian Clarke's 'Catrin' and get a general understanding of the poem.
2 Once you have a general understanding of the poem, re-read it. This time make notes and annotations according to the question.
3 Underline any words or phrases that you don't understand.

WORKIT!

'Environmental blank' – at first glance, this might be an unusual phrase. However, when we look at the words in context, we can see they describe the hospital room in which Catrin was born. We can guess that the room was bare and clean. Surprisingly, there is little emotion involved.

Structure and form

Look at the way the poem is built and gather some information about the structure and form.

- What form does the poem take?
- Write down the number of stanzas.
- Count the number of lines in each stanza and work out one or two line lengths by counting syllables. This will help you to think about rhythm.
- Does the poem rhyme?
- Remember, you need to explain **why** the poet has chosen to use this structural device. For example:

WORKIT!

'Catrin' is made up of a series of short lines. The poem seems to have a stuttering rhythm. The broken rhythm seems to echo the conflict in the relationship. However, each short line leads into the next, suggesting the bond between mother and child.

Imagery

You should think about how the poet uses:

- sight
- sound
- smell
- touch.

Are these images grouped around a particular idea or theme?

For example:

> Red rope of love which we both
> Fought over

Here, the poet is asking us to feel the rope which both are fighting over. It is a sensory detail which makes the relationship vivid.

Language

Highlight any interesting words or groups of words. Think about **why** the poet has decided to use the words you have highlighted. For example:

WORKIT!

> In the glass tank clouded with feelings

...makes it seem as if the mother and the child are surrounded and maybe trapped by their relationship.

DOIT!

Choose three of your annotations from the Do it! on page 144 and develop them into fully written paragraphs. Make sure you give evidence for your ideas by using a short quotation in each paragraph.

Terminology

Look for any poetic techniques that the poet might use, such as:

- Simile: this is a comparison where the poet uses 'as' or 'like'. For example, 'The man was as old as the hills'.

- Metaphor: this makes a strong image in the reader's head. When a poet uses a metaphor, they are saying that a person, place, animal or thing *is* something else. For example, 'The man was a mountain'.

- Personification: a poet might give human attributes to inanimate objects. Objects are given feelings and thoughts. For example, 'The mountain looked out across the country with the wisdom of an old man'.

- Alliteration: when a poet repeats the same sounds they are using alliteration. 'Miraculously the mountain managed to mangle its face into that of a moody man.'

- Onomatopoeia: words which sound like the thing they describe can be very effective in poetry. There are obvious examples like 'bang' and 'crash', but also a word like 'rock' could be said to have a hard and brittle sound like the qualities of the object it describes.

- Repetition: poets sometimes use repetition for emphasis. For example, 'His lonely words echo around the hard and tough, the hard and rough mountain'.

It's not enough to spot techniques: you need to explain why the poet has used these techniques. For example:

WORKIT!

'Catrin' uses one powerful extended metaphor. The rope is an image of the bond that ties mother and daughter. It is powerful because it can represent both safety and restraint.

Themes

Make a list of two or three themes in the poem. For example:

WORKIT!

A central theme in 'Catrin' is the relationship between mother and daughter.

The viewpoint and attitude of the poet

You should think about the persona (the character) of the mother.

- What is her attitude towards her daughter?
- Does she consider the attitude of her daughter in return?
- Do you think the poet and the mother are the same person?
- What does the poet have to say about the relationship between mother and daughter?
- Does the viewpoint of the poet change through the poem?

DOIT!

Read the four paragraphs below written by students. Put them into a rank order. Which do you think is the best and why? Imagine you are the teacher; give each student some feedback.

WORKIT!

Student answer A	The poem uses little assonance, even though this is a fascinating and eloquent poetic device. Therefore, structurally, the poem could be said to be irregular. It has the tone perhaps of a ballad but is devoid of simile, onomatopoeia or other poetic artifice. A fascinating and charming evocation of the relationship between a mother and daughter.
Student answer B	It's like the relationship between the mother and the daughter changes during the poem. At the start the language is quite hard, 'Fierce confrontation' is not the way a mother usually talks about the birth of her daughter. By the end of the poem, it seems like the mother has come to accept that the daughter must have her independence. I think this is good parenting.
Student answer C	The mother seems to be very honest about her relationship with the daughter. The rope is a metaphor for the way that their love for each other holds them together. This is a struggle; it stops both of them being independent. The final image, 'As you ask may you skate in the dark, for one more hour' is very powerful. A mother needs to allow her daughter to be separate but she is frightened of what might happen if she lets go.
Student answer D	I can't remember being born, but my dad showed me a photo once of me just after I was born. He let me have it and said he didn't need it. It got smudged with chocolate by my brother.

Comparing the unseen poems

In the exam, you will be asked to compare another poem with the first poem you have looked at.

A Memory

I remember
The crackle of the palm trees
Over the mooned white roofs of the town…
The shining town…
5 And the tender fumbling of the surf
On the sulphur-yellow beaches
As we sat… a little apart… in the close-pressing night.

The moon hung above us like a golden mango,
And the moist air clung to our faces,
10 Warm and fragrant as the open mouth of a child
And we watched the out-flung sea
Rolling to the purple edge of the world,
Yet ever back upon itself…
15 As we…

Inadequate night…
And mooned white memory
Of a tropic sea…
How softly it comes up
Like an ungathered lily.

Lola Ridge

DO IT!

Use the same method to look at the second unseen poem. Read, re-read and annotate it, thinking about:

- making sense of the poem
- its structure
- its imagery
- its language
- its themes
- the poet's viewpoint and attitude.

As you read, think about the differences and the similarities. The poems will be chosen so that there is plenty to compare. Time is limited, so you only have three or four minutes to make your annotations before writing.

DO IT!

Give yourself three minutes to make your annotations. The copy of the poem below has some annotations to help you.

A Memory

I remember
The **crackle** of the palm trees
Over the mooned white roofs of the town...
The shining town...
And the **tender fumbling of the surf**
On the sulphur-yellow beaches
As we sat... **a little apart**... in the close-pressing night.

The moon hung above us **like a golden mango**,
And the **moist air clung to our faces**,
Warm and fragrant as the open mouth of a child
And **we** watched the out-flung sea
Rolling to the purple edge of the world,
Yet ever back upon itself...
As we**...**

Inadequate night...
And mooned white memory
Of a tropic sea...
How softly it comes up
Like an ungathered lily.

Lola Ridge

1 The poet uses the sense of sound.

2 A tropical setting in contrast to the hospital room at the beginning of Clarke's poem.

3

4

5 Poet draws on sense of touch, Clarke's poem looks closely at emotional feeling.

6 The two people are together in the relationship, the mother and daughter are often in conflict in Clarke's poem.

7

DO IT!

Copy and complete the table below, filling it with your ideas about 'Catrin' and 'A Memory'.

When you have completed your table, leave it for a day or two and then re-read it. Add a few more notes.

Poem	Making sense	Structure	Imagery	Language	Themes	Viewpoint and attitude
'Catrin'	Looks at the bond between a mother and daughter		Use of varied and vibrant colours		A mother's need to care for her daughter	At first distant – like viewing an old photo but by the end the mother is concerned with the present
'A Memory'				Lots of physical words: out-flung, clung, crackle		Nostalgia for a perfect past moment

In addition to AO1 and AO2, exam markers will be interested in the following for comparison questions:

SNAP IT!

	Band 2	Band 3	Band 4	Band 5	Band 6
Comparison between texts	The student's answer... • makes a comparison between poems	The student's answer... • makes a couple of comparisons between the poems' methods and their effects	The student's answer... • makes clear comparisons between the poems in terms of their methods and effects	The student's answer... • makes thoughtful comparisons between the poems in terms of their methods and effects	The student's answer... • explores convincing comparisons between the poems in terms of their methods and effects
Subject terminology	• uses some subject terminology.	• uses some relevant terminology.	• uses some relevant subject terminology.	• uses relevant subject terminology effectively to support points.	• uses relevant subject terminology very precisely to support points.

Mark scheme

The exam marker will be using mark schemes to help grade your work. You will see from the example mark scheme on page 151 that:

The best answers will explore the poem with a critical and well-structured argument. They will use relevant quotations to show insight and develop their own ideas about the poem. They will write in detail about language and structure using the correct terminology.

Weaker answers will tend to retell what happens in the poem. They may provide some reference to the poem and use some examples and quotations. They may use some terminology, but they will tend to identify this and not explain it in any detail.

SNAPIT!

Descriptors	Band 2	Band 3	Band 4	Band 5	Band 6
AO1 Read, understand and respond Use evidence	The student's answer… • is relevant and backs up ideas with references to the text • makes some comments about these references	The student's answer… • sometimes explains the text in relation to the task • refers to details in the text to back up points	The student's answer… • clearly explains the text in relation to the task • uses textual references effectively to back up points	The student's answer… • thoughtfully explains the text in relation to the task • thoughtfully builds appropriate references into points	The student's answer… • critically explores the text in relation to the task • chooses precise textual details to clinch points
AO2 Language, form and structure Subject terminology	• mentions some of the writer's methods • uses some subject terminology.	• comments on some of the writer's methods and their effects • uses some relevant terminology.	• clearly explains the writer's key method, and their effects • helpfully uses varied, relevant terminology.	• thoughtfully explains the writer's key methods and their effects • makes thoughtful use of relevant terminology.	• analyses the writer's key methods, and *how* these influence the reader • chooses subject terminology to make points precise and convincing.

To develop your skills, get used to reading and thinking about poems regularly:

- Read a poem a day.
- Look for poems on the internet.
- Find poems in poetry anthologies in the library.
- Search for poems by a poet you have enjoyed studying.
- Study and analyse song or rap lyrics – they use similar techniques.
- Read and study poems from the other cluster in the anthology (the one you haven't studied) and treat them as unseen poems. There will be plenty to say about these poems – they have been chosen because they are thematically linked.

Once you have selected some unseen poems, make up your own questions by adapting the ones below:

> In [name of poem], how does the poet present the speaker's feelings about [a theme/idea/attitude] in the poem?
>
> In both [name of poem 1] and [name of poem 2] the speakers describe their [feelings/attitudes/ideas]. What are the similarities and/or differences between the ways the poets present those [feelings/attitudes/ideas]?

NAILIT!

In the real exam, you need to prepare your comparison very quickly. Remember you need to:

- read the poem and annotate it
- prepare your comparison
- write your answer.

CHECKIT! ✓

1 How many poems must you write about in the unseen poetry question?

2 How long should you allow to do this section?

3 What language technique(s) is/are used in this line from the poem 'A Memory'?

> " The moon hung above us like a golden mango, "

1 How long is Paper 1?
2 How long should you spend on the Shakespeare question?
3 About how many words will be in the 19th-century extract printed on the exam paper?
4 How long is Paper 2?
5 How many extracts from your modern novel or play will be printed on the exam paper?
6 What is meant by 'an integrated quotation'?
7 How long should you spend writing about your modern novel or play?
8 How long should you spend on the poetry anthology question?
9 What is a metaphor?
10 What is alliteration?
11 What is meant by 'a theme'?
12 In the poetry anthology question, how many poems will you be asked to write about?
13 If your exam board has an 'unseen poetry' section, what does 'unseen' mean?
14 How many unseen poems will you have to write about?
15 How much time should you spend on the unseen poetry question?

Glossary

adjective   A word that describes a noun (for example: a *big* dog; a *good* idea).

adverb   A word that modifies the meaning of a verb, an adjective or another adverb (for example: I run *quickly*; the garden is *quite* pretty; I run *very* quickly).

adverbial   A word or phrase that gives more information about a verb. Usually the information is about where, when or how something happened (for example: He looked *under* the bed. She arrived *last week*. They did it *without any fuss*).

alliteration   Words starting with the same *sound* that the writer has placed near each other for effect (for example: the **b**ig, **b**lue **b**us; one **k**ick **c**aused **ch**aos).

apostrophe   It can be used for two purposes: to show that one or more letters have been missed out (for example: can't, they're, he's); to show possession (for example: Sarah's pen).

argument   A point of view that is explained and defended. An argument in an essay can be an exploration of both sides of a point of view.

autobiography   Writing about a person's life written by that person. 'Autobiography' is an old Greek word that in direct translation means 'self-life writing'.

biography   Writing about someone else's life.

character   A person in a play or story: a person created by the writer.

characterisation   This is about how a character has been written by the author; how the author presents the character so that we see them in a particular way.

clause   See main clause and subordinate clause.

coherence   How a whole text is structured and brought together.

cohesion   How details in a text join together. For example, through the use of connectives and other cohesive ties.

cohesive tie   Another term for a discourse marker.

colloquial language   Informal language that is normally used in speech rather than writing (for example: 'They're out' rather than 'They are not at home'; 'yeah' rather than 'yes').

colon   (:) A punctuation mark used to introduce a list, a quotation or an explanation of something. Also used in place of the phrase 'that is to say' or 'in other words'.

comma   (,) A punctuation mark used as a pause in a sentence to make meaning clear. It is also used to separate words in a list.

complement   The complement of a sentence is its *completion*. The complement completes the sense of the sentence or part of it. The complements in these two sentences are in italics: He was *unhappy*. She made *me worried.*

complex sentence   A sentence with at least one subordinate clause.

conjunction   A word that joins main clauses into one sentence, or joins subordinate clauses to main clauses. Conjunctions include: *when, because, and, but, or, while, although, if, unless.*

connective   This word is sometimes used to refer to a conjunction or other discourse marker.

connotation   The implied meaning of a word of phrase. For example, the word *mob* means a large group of people, but it *connotes* violence. If someone *dashes* down the road, we know that they are moving quickly, but that choice of word also connotes urgency. A connotation is sometimes called a nuance.

context   The context of a poem, play, novel or story is the set of conditions in which it was written. These might include: the writer's life; society, habits and beliefs at the time they wrote; an event that influenced the writing; and the genre of the writing. The context is also seen in terms of influences on the reader, so for example, a modern audience would see a Shakespeare play differently from audiences in his own time, as their life experiences would be different.

deduce   To work something out for yourself, using clues.

dialogue   The words that characters say in plays or in fiction. In fiction, these words are usually shown within inverted commas ('…').

discourse marker   Words and phrases used to join ideas or to change topics and move an argument on: 'Despite this…'; 'Finally…'; 'On the other hand…'; 'This belief is also…'.

effect   The impact that a writer's words have on a reader: how the words create a mood, feeling or reaction.

emotive language   Words chosen to make a reader feel a particular way about something (for example: 'Poor, hungry, little mites' or 'Great, hulking bullies').

enjambement   When a line of poetry does not end with punctuation, but instead its sense runs straight into the next line.

evaluate   To explain how good (or bad) something is: how well it does something. When we evaluate a text we consider ways in which it is successful (or unsuccessful), and the impact it has on us.

evidence   Details or clues that support a point of view. A quotation can be a form of evidence in which a few words are copied from a text to support a point of view.

explicit   Explicit information is clearly stated; it's on the surface of a text and should be obvious.

fiction   Novels or stories made up by an author.

grammar   Grammar is the system and structure of language: how words are put together to make sense and be effective. The 'rules' of grammar can change over time, and so 'conventions' would be a better term than 'rules'. Grammar covers word classes (including verbs, nouns, adjectives) and sentence elements (for example: subject, object, complement, clause, phrase, and so on).

iambic (pentameter)   A 'beat' in poetry, when syllables alternate between unstressed and stressed (for example: I **walked** a**long** the **stor**my **shore** with **Jane**). An iambic pentameter is a line with five of these unstressed/stressed patterns in a row (as in the example).

imagery   The 'pictures' a writer puts into the reader's mind. Similes and metaphors are particular forms of imagery. We also talk about violent, graphic, religious imagery, and so on.

implicit (imply)   Implicit information is only suggested (or implied), it is not stated directly; we have to infer to understand it. The opposite of explicit.

infer (inference)   To 'read between the lines'; to work out meaning from clues in the text. See implicit. When we infer, we are making an inference.

interpret   To work out meaning, using clues and evidence. The same piece of writing can be interpreted in different ways, but evidence has to support interpretations.

language (choices)   The words and the style that a writer chooses in order to have an effect on a reader.

main clause   The main part of a sentence, including a verb and often an object (for example: *The cat caught a mouse*). The main clause often makes sense on its own.

metaphor   Comparing two things by referring to them as though they are the same thing (for example: His face *was a thunder cloud*. The boy *was an angry bear*).

narrator   The person who tells the story. A *first person narrator* tells the story as though it is happening to them personally (for example: '*I* walked slowly down the street'). A *third person narrator* tells the story from someone else's point of view (for example: '*He* walked slowly down the street').

non-fiction   Texts that are not made up (for example: textbooks, encyclopaedias, information leaflets, speeches, shopping lists).

noun   A word used to identify people, places or things (a common noun – for example: *boy, bridge, train*) or to name a particular one of these (proper noun – *Sophie, Liverpool, Westminster Abbey*).

nuance   Implied meaning: see connotation.

object   The thing in the sentence that 'receives' the action (the verb). In the following sentences the object is in italics: He poured *the tea*. She ate *her breakfast*.

onomatopoeia   A word whose meaning is in its sound (for example: *smash, crash, plop*).

oxymoron   Two normally contradictory words next to each other (for example: 'Burning ice'; 'miserable happiness').

paragraph   A section of writing. A new paragraph is shown by leaving a line space between sentences or by starting a sentence in from the margin. New paragraphs show a change of time, topic, speaker or place.

personification   A metaphor that represents a thing as a living creature (for example: the waves were *leaping white horses.* The storm *threatened* the town).

perspective   Another term for viewpoint. Our perspective is how we 'see' things.

phrase   A group of words that do a job together in a sentence (for example: he looked *under the bed*).

playwright   The writer of a play.

plot   The plot of a literary text is the *story* – the narrative – or an interrelated series of events as described by the author.

preposition   A word that shows the physical relationship between two things (for example: *in, through, under, on, between, over*).

pronoun   A word that stands in place of a noun, a noun phrase or pronoun (for example: *I/ me, we/us, he/him, she/her, they/them, it, mine, ours, theirs, myself, themselves, and so on*).

quotation   A word, phrase, sentence or passage copied from a text, usually used to support an argument or point of view. A quotation should be surrounded by inverted commas ('…'). It is usually wise to make quotations as short as possible, sometimes just one well-chosen word is enough.

register   The style and tone of a text. Registers can range from very formal and technical to highly informal, even insulting. Using the right register is a key skill in English.

rhetorical question   A question in a text, or particularly in speech, for which no answer is expected (for example: *How many times do I have to tell you? How many times must we go through this before we see the error of our ways?*)

rhyme   Words chosen by a poet because they finish with the same sound (for example: *he/flea; stable/label; laughter/after*).

rhythm   The 'beat' in poetry or music.

semicolon   (;) A punctuation mark sometimes used instead of a full stop when the two sentences either side of the semicolon explain each other (for example: *He was sad; he cried*). It is often used instead of the word 'because'. A semicolon suggests a slightly longer pause in a sentence than a comma.

sentence   A group of words that together can stand on their own and make complete sense. It starts with a capital letter and ends with either a full stop, question mark or exclamation mark. A sentence contains or implies a predicate and a subject. Sentences can be very short, very long, or somewhere in between.

setting   The setting is the *time and place* in which a play or story takes place. The setting could also include the social and political circumstances (or context) of the action.

simile   Comparing two things using either the word *like* or *as* (for example: The boy was *like an angry bear*. His running was *as loud as thunder*. Her face was *as yellow as custard*).

simple sentence   A complete sentence with just one verb (or verb chain). A simple sentence can still be long.

slang   Informal language (for example: *kid* rather than child; *grub* rather than food; *guys* rather than people).

soliloquy   A speech made by a character in a play to the audience only – not to another character. Soliloquies are rarely used nowadays, but they are common in Shakespeare's plays. They can be a good way of allowing the audience to 'hear' what a character is thinking and feeling.

stanza   A verse of a poem.

structural features   Features used by a writer to give their writing shape and coherence. These are the features that hold writing together. Structural features include: tone, style, repetitions, extended images, shifts of focus, voice and viewpoint, openings and closings, sequencing of ideas, links between paragraphs and sentences.

structure   How a text is organised and held together: all those things that shape a text and make it coherent. See cohesion and coherence.

style   Writing styles can vary between writers, or writers may use different styles at different times (for example: they might sometimes write informally with energy, while in other texts they might write formally, creating a style that gives them an air of authority). Style and tone are closely related.

subject   The 'do-er' of a sentence (for example, in the following sentences the subject is in italics: *He* ran quickly. *Jane* saw the accident. *The cat* was bored).

subject terminology   The technical words that are used for a particular subject. All the words in this glossary are subject terminology for English.

subordinate clause   Part of the sentence that cannot stand on its own, but gives more information about the main clause. A subordinate clause always contains a subject and a verb. The subordinate clause is set in italics in the sentence: He walked quickly *because he was late.*

summarise   Reduce the content of a text to its essentials (for example: when you explain to a friend what happened in a film).

synthesise   Bring information together from different sources to make a coherent whole. See coherence.

technique   Another word for method. Writers use different techniques to create different effects.

tense (verb)   See verb. Verbs can be used in various forms (or tenses) to indicate *when* something happened. For example, something that happened in the past, is happening now (present) or will happen (future). Tense shows *when* an action took place. For example, *I run* (present), *I ran* (past), *I will run* (future).

theme   A theme is a central idea in a text. Common themes in novels, films, poems and other literary texts include: loyalty, love, race, betrayal, poverty, good versus evil, and so on.

tone   The mood of a text, or the attitude of the author or narrator towards the topic. Tones can be mocking, affectionate, polite, authoritative, and so on.

verb   A *doing*, *being* or *having* word: for example, *run, am, have.*

viewpoint   A writer's or character's point of view: their attitudes, beliefs and opinions.

vocabulary   The words a writer chooses to use. They might use a particular sort of vocabulary (for example: formal, simple or shocking).

voice (narrative)   A written account of connected events can be neutral in opinion. Sometimes a writer's attitude and tone is much more noticeable – as though you can 'hear' them. This is the writer's voice.

Answers

ENGLISH LANGUAGE
Fiction: Reading

AO1

Do it! (p.11)

Answer 2 is wrong because the boy's fair hair is not caused by the heat, and therefore it is not relevant.

Answer 3 is wrong because 'smashed' and 'anger' might often be connected to heat, but they are not necessarily connected here.

Check it! (p.12)

1 Finding the information.
2 Explicit information is information that is right there in front of us. Implicit information is information that is suggested or implied.

AO2

Do it! (p.14)

Answers could include:

Shorter sentences give a sort of punchline effect. This is most apparent at the end: the final sentence is not even a whole sentence because it has no verb and only means something in the context of the previous sentence. It seems to sum up the narrator's disgust and disappointment in a very direct way.

Do it! (p.16)

Answer	How it compares with the mark scheme descriptors	Mark band
A	The student chooses one relevant quotation and gives a very brief explanation of what it tells us about the narrator, although nothing is said about how it affects the mood of the extract, and not much detail is offered in the explanation. However, there is some understanding of language choice and how this conveys meaning.	2
B	The student's answer is perceptive: they infer intelligently from precise details in the text. The analysis is deft and takes account of nuances, vocabulary and sentence forms. The answer uses a range of relevant terminology – impression, swear word, sentence – to precisely identify methods and their effects on the reader.	4

Do it! (p.16)

Example of a simple sentence:

'Miguel was there already.'

Example of compound sentence:

'I left the 'welcome' desk and dragged my bags angrily for the next half hour up to my room.'

Example of complex sentence:

'There were two flights of steep steps to negotiate before I could reach my assigned hovel on the third storey of the dilapidated building.'

The effect the sentence forms on the reader shows the narrator was unhappy with his new accommodation:

- Sarcastic inverted commas around 'welcome' (to show he did not find the hotel welcoming).
- He is angry.
- He chooses to include the detail of how far up and inconvenient his room is.
- He calls his room a 'hovel'.
- The room is cramped.
- He has a roommate who takes more than his fair share of space in the room.
- His roommate is covering the narrator's part of the room with germs.

Do it! (p.17)

Answer will be a personal response.

Do it! (p.18)

A bike – e.g. chain, two wheels, spokes, handlebars.

A school – e.g. timetable, teachers, rules, lessons.

A film – e.g. characters, plot, climax, shots.

An extract from a novel – e.g. paragraphs, dialogue, descriptions, characters, an event, tone of writing.

Do it! (p.20)

- Briony is controlling and very neat and precise. She leaves nothing to chance. She likes order. She likes to be in charge.
- Lists, long sentences, precise details, very precise adjective choices.
- Smaller structural features help the writer to build that impression of Briony. For example, the linking phrase 'in fact' shows the narrator is going to emphasise something they have already explained – her tidiness. 'in fact' links the first and second halves of the paragraphs.

Do it! (p.21)

Answer A: Band 3; Answer B: Band 4; Answer C: Band 2.

Check it! (p.22)

1 See page 14 for the key words.
2 See page 19 for a list of structural features.
3 Repetitions, although almost anything could be a structural feature if it is deliberately used to give the text shape and meaning.
4 Any three from: change of topic, place, time or speaker.
5 A man as a duck.
6 The attitude of the writer or narrator to what is being written about: for example, mocking, serious, sympathetic.
7 The features that hold it together, make it 'work', and make it recognisable as narrative fiction.

AO4

Do it! (p.24)

Other possible and equally reasonable reactions to the *Sons and Lovers* extract:

'We really sympathise with Miriam, even though we sense that she is a strong character.'

'Paul and Miriam seem so different from each other: she is very anxious, but he seems to be insensitive.'

Do it! (p.25)

Here is an example of what a student said about the writing:

I get the impression that the narrator is fed up and deflated. The writer's choice of words is effective at giving this impression: he 'drags' his bags up the stairs to what he calls his 'assigned hovel'. He sounds like he is unhappy at having no choice of room, which he chooses to call a 'hovel'. This is his judgement, not presumably the official description of the room. The last sentence is just two words, the second one repeating the word at the end of the previous sentence. It makes him sound like he is very miserable and defeated. The writing is good because mostly it just hints at the narrator's feelings.

I also get the impression that he feels let down...

Do it! (p.26)

Answers will be a personal response.

Check it! (p.28)

1 See the golden rules on pages 23–4.

2 B, C, A. However, C could be considered to be at least as good as B, just less conventional in its approach. B chooses a wider range of relevant quotations to justify views. C is much stronger on personal response, and the response is valid and considered. There is no depth to answer A: it does not explain points and evidence, and it does not consider what is good about the writing. It tries simply to stick to 'facts' in the text.

3 How well does the writer create comedy in this extract?

Review it! (p.29–30)

1 15 minutes

2 Read the questions and mark useful, relevant bits of the text as you read it.

3 Whether you can find the information that is actually there in front of you: facts.

4 Any four from:
- Hamid was running.
- He was in too much of a hurry to finish using the toilet.
- He grabbed a weapon (and was ready to kill with it).
- His wife was screeching.
- Rupban has stopped plucking the chicken.
- Mumtaz wouldn't let Hamid stop.
- She gave him an urgent instruction (not a request).
- She is sarcastic and insulting to him to sting him into action.

5 The effects of the writer's structural and language choices.

6 Some possibilities include:
- Clipped language ('See', 'perfect everywhere') suggests she is harsh, insensitive.
- Grand metaphor to suggest her own grandness: 'ease her path to this world'.
- Aside – 'she should have strangled them at birth' - reveals her selfish ruthlessness.
- 'Of course' suggests generosity, but her real motives are then revealed, suggesting dishonesty.

7 Any ten from:
- Information put into a particular order (sequence).
- Dialogue to reveal character, move the narrative on, and so on.
- Narrative chronology.
- Narrative shifts.
- Repetition – of words, phrases, ideas, images, and so on.
- Changing/developing focus.
- Extended images.
- A particular style, tone or mood.
- Narrative voice and perspective.
- Paragraphs.
- Summaries, introductions, conclusions.

8 Some possibilities include:
- A sequence of events, one leading to the next.
- Dialogue (and implied dialogue) to act as a sort of commentary on the sequence of events.
- Words consistently chosen to communicate physical feelings very clearly – 'slick', 'yowl', 'explosions', 'spittle', 'yelled', named colours.

9 To consider how successful the writer has been in engaging the reader.

10 Answers will vary but make sure you can justify your feelings with evidence from the text.

11 Answers should:
- show understanding of the mark scheme
- express your thoughts and feelings about how Banesa is presented in the extracts
- explain how the writer has created these thoughts and feelings.

Fiction: Writing

Do it! (p.34)

B – It is narrative fiction because it is written in the past tense (for example, 'caught' – not 'catches') and it contains dramatic action: someone seems to be preparing to attack the hotel in some way. In addition, it is written in the third person (she). If you described a day in your life you would be writing in the first person (I).

Check it! (p.35)

1 40 marks

2 24 marks

3 AQA, Edexcel and OCR offer the choice of two tasks. Eduqas offer the choice of four.

4 See page 33.

Question type 1: descriptive writing with a visual stimulus

Do it! (p.37)

Answers will be a personal response.

Check it! (p.39)

1   For example:

The castle doesn't care any more. It sticks its tongue out rudely at us, but we know it doesn't really mean it: its face is as serene as the lake that surrounds it. The lake is the castle's very own vanity mirror. The old brickwork squats and waits. It has learned to be patient. It has all the time in the world. Still, it does yearn for the old days when armoured knights, not brightly coloured tourists, streamed through its interior.

simile, **metaphor**, personification.

Question type 2: descriptive writing without a visual stimulus

Do it! (p.41)

Answer will be a personal response.

Do it! (p.42)

Answer will be a personal response.

Do it! (p.42)

Most people (and markers) would probably find answer B better because it is much more engaging: the opening is dramatic and grabs our attention. Answer A spends most of the time explaining what the student *will* write. Answer B just gets on with it. If we look at the mark scheme on p.35 we see that answer B is 'engaging' and chooses vocabulary for 'deliberate effect' on the reader. In fact, this answer is probably heading towards Band 4.

Do it! (p.43)

*   The castle is sandy brown in the mid-afternoon light.
*   Its drawbridge is like an outstretched tongue.

Check it! (p.44)

1   Annotating the question means marking up the question with notes to make sure you understand and do exactly what it is telling you to do. It also helps you to remember your ideas.

2   Planning involves thinking through the structure, the content and the language for your writing.

3   The opening of your writing should engage your reader effectively and in an appropriate way.

4   A is the better opening because it is less factual and more interesting. The description is creative and uses ambitious language.

5   c and e

Question type 3: narrative with a visual stimulus

Check it! (p.47)

1   'Thinking outside the box' for this question could mean asking yourself:
    *   What might be (happening) just outside the picture?
    *   What could explain what is in the picture?
    *   What people in the picture might be thinking and feeling.

2   Characters

Question type 4: narrative writing – the opening to a story

Do it! (p.49)

Answers will be a personal response.

Do it! (p.50)

A sets the mood and atmosphere.

B addresses the reader directly.

C starts with dialogue before setting a dramatic mood.

Do it! (p.50)

Red-faced and grunting, Harry stamped his foot on the accelerator, revving the engine, but only spinning his wheels hopelessly in the sticky mud.

He lay scrunched by the rock that had tripped him, a red pool forming by his outstretched hand.

The dog barked and spun in this strange white world.

Check it! (p.50)

1   a   Setting mood and atmosphere; raises questions about who she is and what she is up to; description of setting.

    b   A hook that causes the reader to raise questions or surprises the reader.

    c   A hook that addresses the reader directly.

2   For example: He stumbled over the kerb.

3   Many elements could be used, including the seven narrative hooks.

Question type 5: narrative writing – a complete story

Do it! (p.53)

1   Normality: the beginning of the story.

    Disruption/problem: drinking.

    Climax/crisis: setting off the fireworks and going back to one that did not go off.

    Return to normality/result: life-changing injuries/ beginning to adjust to a new normality.

2   a   In the middle of Band 3.

    b   The writing is fairly 'clear, effective and engaging' and chooses language 'for effect'. However, the register becomes too loose and that damages the tension, and there are few examples of careful crafting of language.

Check it! (p.53)

1 You will write more convincingly about situations you know or understand.

2 Normality

Disruption/problem

Climax/crisis

Return to normality/result

3 Too much dialogue and a clichéd ending such as, 'I woke up and it was all a dream.'

Review it! (p.54)

1 AQA, Edexcel and OCR offer the choice of two tasks. Eduqas offer the choice of four.

2 See page 33.

3 40%

4 Any of: past tense, characters, action, fiction

5 At least 45 minutes

6 5–10 minutes

7 Any of: metaphor, simile, personification, image

8 A man as a train

9 Turning it into narrative writing.

10 Describing an event.

11 A: the complete version would read, 'I smelt a delicious aroma of chocolate.'

12 Engage the reader (in an appropriate way).

13 Any of the following:

- A hook that sets the mood and atmosphere.
- A hook that causes the reader to raise questions or surprises the reader.
- A hook that focuses on a character.
- A hook that starts with a key event or action.
- A hook which addresses the reader directly.
- A hook that begins with dialogue.
- A hook that describes the setting.

14 Showing allows readers to work something out for themselves, which is what we have to do in real life.

15 For example:

She smiled at Zanira. 'I know you want the last piece of pizza, but I'm afraid it's got my name written all over it, and my need is greater than yours.'

16 Normality, Disruption/problem, Climax/crisis, Return to normality/result

Non-fiction: Reading

AO1

Do it! (p.57)

1 In answers E and F, the only aspect of inference is that we have to realise that 'insane' and 'mad', and 'unnecessary' and 'no need' are synonyms.

Check it! (p.59)

1 • Sometimes you have to work out (infer) information.

- Answer the questions accurately.
- Use the information in the texts.

2 Some true statements that could be used by exam markers for the extract about 'Let it Go':

- Children like 'Let it Go'.
- Very young children like the song a lot.
- The writer cannot remember another song that has been adopted so enthusiastically by very young children.
- The writer thinks that pop music makes lovers seem fickle.

AO2

Do it! (p.62)

1 Here is the opening of one student's answer to this question:

For most of us family is very important, and presumably Chief Seattle expects family to be important to the president, so he presents parts of the environment he wants to save as family members: for example,...

Check it! (p.63)

1 • Explain your views, and use some evidence.

- Use some subject terminology.
- Analyse the effect of the writer's choice of language and structure. (Not structure for AQA.)

2 The main focus is the writer's use of language and structure and its effects on the reader. (Not structure for AQA.)

3 For example: repetitions, echoing of words and phrases, clear, poetic noun phrases.

4 For example:

- Repetitions are for emphasis and to make his letter sound like a rhetorical speech: '<u>Every</u> part of this earth is sacred to my people. <u>Every</u> shining pine needle, <u>every</u> humming insect.'
- Echoing of words and phrases also creates a hypnotic rhythm for the letter: 'We know the sap which <u>courses</u> through the trees as we know the blood that <u>courses</u> through our veins. We are <u>part</u> of the earth and it is <u>part</u> of us.'
- Clear, poetic noun phrases inspire the reader: 'the freshness of the air'; 'the sparkle of the water'; 'the clear waters of the lakes'.

AO3

Do it! (p.65)

See page 64.

Do it! (p.65)

1 Answers will be a personal response.

2 Notice the different styles of the titles and the different feelings they give us about cauliflowers. Use this in your answer.

Do it! (p.68)

Answer will be a personal response.

Do it! (p.70)

Answer will be a personal response.

Check it! (p.71)

1 Two

2 Language

3 About 180 words, but making precise points supported by evidence is more important.

4 Paragraph 2: nature and people.

Paragraph 3: family and ancestors.

Paragraph 4: land is sacred.

Paragraph 5: Mother Earth.

Paragraph 6: we depend on the Earth.

Paragraph 7: you depend on the Earth.

Paragraph 8: keep our spirit.

Paragraph 9: we are dependent on the Earth and on one another: we are all deeply interconnected.

Check it! (p.75)

1 See page 73.

2 Some advice for the student who wrote the sample answer:

This is a strong answer. It identifies some effective techniques in the writing, why readers might like it, and how it might motivate them (impact). Evidence from different parts of the text is chosen to illustrate points – especially about tone and effect. The comment about 'suppers' being a bad choice of word is based your own lack of knowledge though, so be careful about any sort of criticism. To reach the top band, perhaps you should start with an overview in which you answer the whole question. For example: 'Lawson's recipe is effective because it gives both clear instructions and uses creative, playful language. In this way it helps would-be cooks, but also gives under-confident cooks encouragement'.

3 This answer is near the top of Band 3.

Review it! (p.76)

1 About 1 hour

2 1, except for Edexcel. For Edexcel both texts will have been written after 1900.

3 b

4 c

5 b

6 Suitable words and phrases include:

On the one hand…

Whereas

While

Similarly

In the same way

Different

By contrast

By comparison

However

But.

7 1

8 d (AQA will not ask you about structure)

9 The quotations from the text are an example of evidence from the text. 'A sequence of personal pronouns' is an example of subject terminology.

10 Communicate or send.

11 c

12 Rhetorical questions. They lead the reader to agree automatically with the writer because only one answer is possible. The rhetorical question tries to stop the reader from thinking about other perspectives on the problem.

Non-fiction: Writing

Check it! (p.78)

1 40 marks

2 16 marks

3 AQA offers one task. Edexcel and OCR will offer a choice of two tasks. The Eduqas paper will have two tasks, but you must do them both.

4 explain, instruct/advise, argue, persuade

5 story

Do it! (p.79)

1 Getting the style right for a head teacher:

My friends and I are given a lot of homework. We object to this because it makes us stressed. We already have enough work to do in school. I feel strongly about this. We are asking that teachers should stop setting homework.

Do it! (p.80)

- Relationship: connection (to), interconnection, how we treat…

- Belong: possess, own, property, ours

Do it! (p.80)

1 Preparing the question:

Topic of letter

'School uniform is important because it allows students to focus on their work rather than on fashion.'

What sort of person might think this?

Showing off, self-expression, creativity

Distract, concentrate

Write a letter to the governors at your school, arguing for or against this statement.

For or against – not both

Other useful key words:

persuade

case

point

view(point)

2 Audience: (my school's) governors

Purpose: arguing (for or against)

Form: (formal) letter

Check it! (p.80)

1 Formal English used in official situations.

2 About one minute.

3 Synonyms are different words that mean roughly the same thing. It is useful to have synonyms for key words in the question so that you don't have to keep repeating them. Thinking about synonyms helps you to understand the key words.

Do it! (p.82)

1 Healthy options.

Do it! (p.83)

From best to worst: C, B, A.

A is far too informal and is therefore both inappropriate and ineffective.

Version C might seem a bit long-winded, but it is polite and respectful. By the end of the paragraph, the governors will be willing to read the rest of the letter and give it careful consideration. That is why the opening is effective.

Do it! (p.84)

An exam marker comments:

This letter is well-organised and uses a style and tone that are appropriate for a respectable group like school governors who have to make carefully considered decisions. Perhaps the rather outdated word 'attire' is going too far, and perhaps implying that the governors may be 'patronising' so early in the letter might irritate them unnecessarily. However, the construction of the first main paragraph is a very cunning piece of reader manipulation: it turns governors' supposed opposition to fashion against them: the final sentence implies that it is the governors – not students – who are victims of (old) fashion.

Check it! (p.84)

1 5–10 minutes.

2 Planning means you know what the **content** of your writing and its order will be before you start writing. This allows you to concentrate on how you express yourself.

Do it! (p.87)

a Persuade; b Advise; c Explain; d Argue.

Do it! (p.88)

The point is made forcefully – even rudely here. The language choices are dramatic and emotive: 'crazy', 'terrible', 'just wrong', 'hate'.

The language needs to be more carefully matched to the readers: school governors. The word choices and arguments need to be more sophisticated.

Check it! (p.90)

1 a False

b True

c False

d False

e True: an introduction can be helpful for the reader.

f False. 'Dear Sir' or 'Dear Madam' should sign off with 'Yours faithfully…'.

2 Here are some examples of openings.

a A letter to your head teacher/principal explaining why you need a week off school/college:

Dear Mrs Jones,

I know that the school has a firm policy of not allowing students to take time off during the term. However,...

b A leaflet advising old people on how to stay fit and active:

They say you are never too old to be fit, and there is a great deal of truth in this.

c An article in a free magazine persuading visitors of the advantages of your local area:

Where could you go that is a romantic as Paris, as picturesque as Rome and as reasonably priced as Bournemouth? Well, Bournemouth, of course!

Review it! (p.91–92)

1 Transactional writing is writing that is intended to communicate, persuade or inform.

2 45 minutes for AQA and Edexcel. 1 hour for Eduqas and OCR.

3 Five minutes

4 Audience, purpose, form

5 To state and develop a point of view.

6 To explain; to instruct or advise; to argue; to persuade

7 Formal letter, article, leaflet, speech, essay

8 Purpose: to advise. Form: a leaflet.

9 Organisation and VSSSP

10 A is more formal. It uses formal language and structure. B uses slang terms such as 'safe as anything', 'kids' and 'ok'.

11 Identify the key words; jot down useful synonyms; identify the audience, purpose and form; jot down first thoughts; make sure you understand the requirements of the question.

12 Audience: readers, listeners

Purpose: aim, what it's for, reason for writing

Form: format, genre, type, style, category

13 To reject it; or to show you have considered it; or to sound reasonable.

14 Two from:

- To collect your ideas together.
- To plan a structure for your writing.
- To leave you free to concentrate on style and expression as you write.

15 Lively opening that sounds reassuring. However, it doesn't sound as confident as it might. The use of the word 'you' is wrong, as the audience is teachers of the visitors, while 'you' presumably refers to the students themselves.

16 You need to grab the reader's interest, be clear, and make sure that tone, style and vocabulary are appropriate for the task's given context.

17 The key elements are:
- clear and effective style
- appropriate language choices
- match register to purpose, form and audience
- effective vocabulary
- a range of linguistic devices used well
- detailed and well-connected ideas
- well-organised paragraphs
- effective use of varied structural features.

18 The cool consideration of alternatives, and the lack of dramatic language suggests that this writing is *arguing* a topic. However, this might well be part of an *advice* text.

19 b and e are probably rhetorical questions as they are not genuinely seeking information: instead they are making a point, and no reply is expected.

Writing: VSSSP

Sentence demarcation

Do it! (p.93)

We cannot go on spoiling the planet we live on. **I**n just a few decades we have dug up and burnt the fossil fuels that nature took millions of years to create. **H**ow much longer will we be able to carry on doing this**?** **W**e must stop it now**!** **O**ur children and grandchildren will not thank us for using up all the planet's resources before they are even born.

Do it! (p.94)

Novel extract: **J**avad stretched and yawned. **H**e could hardly keep his eyes open. **H**ow would he ever stay awake until morning and the safety of daylight**?** **H**e had promised to keep watch, but now his will was weakening. **H**e edged a few inches away from the fire. **P**erhaps coldness would fight tiredness. **H**e knew that he and James would both rather be cold than dead**!** *(or .)*

Advertisement extract: **C**ome alive with **Z**ingo **F**izz**!** **Z**ingo **F**izz is the tingling new soft drink that will make you glad to be young. *(or !)* **I**f you're not young, then **Z**ingo will make you think you are. *(or !)* **W**hat could be wrong with that**?** **D**rink **Z**ingo. *(or !)* **I**t's good to be young, even if you're not. *(or !)*

Punctuation

Do it! (p.95)

1 Dashes used instead of brackets for non-essential text that adds extra detail; Comma used to make the reader pause so that a detail can be emphasised; Full stop (Jenny B.) to indicate that letters are missing; Full stop to indicate the end of a sentence; Semicolon which stands before an explanation; Comma used to separate words in a list; Comma used to make meaning clearer.

Do it! (p.95)

1 To make the reader pause so that a detail can be emphasised.

2 To separate words in a list.

3 To make meaning clearer.

Do it! (p.96)

a is incorrectly punctuated. The comma should be a full stop.

b is correct.

c is correct.

d is incorrectly punctuated. The comma should be a full stop.

Do it! (p.97)

a We can't go to Nelum's party because we promised we'd visit our nan's house.

b It's important to eat lots of vegetables.

c The students' (or student's) ideas for raising money were very imaginative.

d Chanelle's idea for raising money was the most popular.

Check it! (p.98)

1 Punctuation can be used to guide and control the reader's reaction or to emphasise certain details for meaning and effect.

2 The three purposes of a comma are: to separate words in a list; to make the reader pause so that a detail can be emphasised; to make meaning clearer.

3 a - Leaping in the air, Sadia neatly caught the ball. The comma is needed to mark the end of a non-finite clause at the beginning of a sentence.

4 a He got up late; he missed the bus.

The semicolon here means 'and therefore'. The two statements explain each other.

b There was a reason he missed the bus: he got up late.

Here the colon is used instead of 'and that was...'

5 I was shocked when I saw his parents' car.

The apostrophe comes straight after the owner or – here – owners.

6 Breathing heavily, I came to a stop outside my destination: the station. I gasped for air; my lungs were bursting. Although I had hardly got my breath back, I forced my legs to take me onto the platform. The train was coming in.

Sentences

Do it! (p.99)

For example: Running quickly, he finally reached the safety of the big rock. He looked back for his pursuers. He couldn't see them. Relieved, he drank some water.

Standard English

Do it! (p.101)

Sentences b, d, e and f use informal English. See below for corrected versions:

b Standard English: <u>John and I</u> went to the beach.

d Standard English: She <u>doesn't</u> like curry.

e Standard English: He was <u>sitting</u> on the wall.

f Standard English: We <u>did</u> it so badly.

Check it (p.102)

1   For effect and impact, and to to show a higher level of language proficiency.

2   For example: I was hungry so I put two samosas in the oven; I was hungry. Therefore I put two samosas in the oven; I was hungry because I put two samosas in the oven; I was hungry when I put two samosas in the oven.

3   A: Band 3; B: Band 4; C: Band 2

Spelling, vocabulary and mark scheme

Check it! (p.105–6)

1   Homophones are words that sound the same but have different meanings and spellings.

2   a – disappear

3   This is the suggested best version: She lay beneath the tree in **agony**, blood **oozing** from the deep **gash** and soaking into the earth around her.

4   **a** • Correct layout for formal letter: address, date, starts correctly with 'Dear'.

   • The opening uses Standard English: After reading about your proposed review of the school's uniform policy, I am writing to share my viewpoint...

   • Ambitious vocabulary is correctly spelled: attire; patronising; Conversely.

   • Sentence structure is used for effect: Although some might argue; Despite many adults' concerns; Moreover.

   • A wide range of punctuation is used: semicolons – Comfort is an essential requirement when focusing on our work; ... Colons – companies have relaxed the need for such clothing in the workplace: ...

   b Here are some important aspects of the mark scheme that apply to this letter:

   • Appropriate Standard English with control and flexibility.

   • Spells almost all words correctly.

   • Wide and adventurous vocabulary.

Review it! (p.107)

1   40%

2   No. It is also about making effective choices of vocabulary, sentences, punctuation.

3   The six aspects are: sentence demarcation, punctuation, sentences, Standard English, spelling, vocabulary.

4   Full stop, exclamation mark, question mark

5   Any seven from: full stop, comma, dash, brackets, semicolon, colon, speech marks, apostrophe, exclamation mark, question mark, ellipsis (...)

6   To make content clear, to guide and control the reader's reaction, and to emphasise certain details for meaning and effect.

7   Sentences b and d use a comma incorrectly.

8   a – The semicolon should be a full stop. *He woke up while it was still dark. He went downstairs.*

9   To introduce some information – usually some sort of list; to mean 'that is to say' or 'in other words'.

10 Every sentence uses at least one apostrophe wrongly. Here is how they should have been written:

   a Sadiq's uncle bought some potatoes.

   b It's hot today.

   c The children's teacher couldn't be found anywhere.

   d I picked up the kettle by its handle.

   e The river's flow wasn't fast enough.

11 Sentence variety is about varying the types of your sentence and the order of their parts to get the best effect and to keep your reader's interest.

12 **This** tiredness stayed with Errol all week. **He** didn't seem to be able to get out of bed. **Even when** Hayley knocked on the door **and** called through the letter box, he just couldn't stir himself. Nights and days slowly passed through his stuffy room like silent visitors. **They** didn't trouble him though. His eyes were closed **and** he was elsewhere in his head. **Because** of his fever, he often didn't really know where he was.

13 c – It should read: *We weren't speaking to each other.*

   Note: a is correct. Many people wrongly say 'She waved to John and I.' This does not make sense because you couldn't say 'She waved to I.' This is not Standard English.

14 independant should be independent; hopefull should be hopeful; neccessary should be necessary; dissappear should be disappear.

ENGLISH LITERATURE

Shakespeare

Do it! (p.114)

Response 2 is better because it offers contextual information that is useful: it improves our understanding of the play.

Check it! (p.116)

All answers will be personal responses.

The 19th-century novel

Check it! (p.122)

1   AQA, Eduqas and OCR: 45 minutes; Edexcel: 55 minutes

2   About 400 words

3   The theme is the central idea in the text: for example, poverty, injustice, marriage, men and women, and so on.

Modern texts

All answers will be personal responses.

Poetry anthology

Check it! (p.142)

1 Individual words

2 Helping your reader to understand the poem.

3 Two poems

Unseen poetry

Do it! (p.143)

Skills and focuses include:

- Analysing the effects of language.
- Quoting to support and clarify your views.
- Spotting key themes.
- Commenting on patterns in the poem – rhyme, rhythm, extended metaphors, etc.

Do it! (p.147)

Rank order from best to worst: C, B, A, C.

Student A: This answer sounds good, but says nothing about the poem, except what it hasn't got!

Student B: Interesting points but nothing is examined precisely: the points are a little vague.

Student C: This answer is more precise and uses evidence to make a clear point.

Student D: This is a charming answer, but completely irrelevant to the question.

Check it! (p.152)

1 Two poems

2 AQA and Edexcel: 45 minutes; Eduqas: 1 hour; OCR: 1 hour 15 minutes

3 Simile

Review it! (p.153)

1 AQA and Edexcel: 1 hour 45 minutes; Eduqas and OCR: 2 hours

2 AQA and Eduqas: 1 hour; Edexcel: 55 minutes; OCR: 45 minutes

3 About 400 words

4 AQA and Edexcel: 2 hours and 15 minutes; Eduqas and OCR: 2 hours

5 None. The question will not focus on one part of the text.

6 One which you build into your own sentence. For example, Macbeth concludes that life is 'a tale told by an idiot.'

7 AQA and Eduqas: 45 minutes; Edexcel: 50 minutes; OCR: 1 hour and 15 minutes

8 AQA: 45 minutes; Edexcel: 35 minutes; Eduqas: 1 hour; OCR: 30 minutes on part (b)

9 Comparing two things by saying they *are* the same: e.g. His face was a big plate.

10 Words near to each other that have been chosen because they start with the same sound: for example, the phone was flat and funky.

11 A central idea or belief that a text explores.

12 Two

13 You won't know in advance what the poems are, and so you will probably not have read them before.

14 Two (OCR will ask you to compare an unseen poem with a poem from the anthology)

15 AQA and Edexcel: 45 minutes; Eduqas: 1 hour; OCR: 45 minutes on part (a)

Index